BERLAGE IN AMSTERDAM

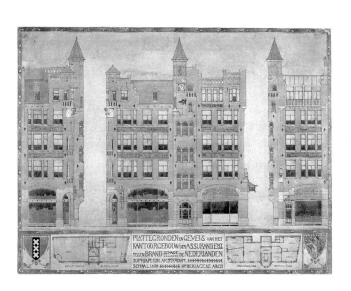

PLATTEGRONDEN en GEVELS van het
KANTOORGEBOUW der ASSURANTIE MI
tegen BRAND SCHADE DE NEDERLANDEN
SOPHIAPLEIN AMSTERDAM
SCHAAL 1:150 H.P.BERLAGE NZ. ARCH

Berlage in Amsterdam

Manfred Bock, Jet Collee
and Hester Coucke

Edited by Maarten Kloos

Architectura & Natura Press

Editor
Maarten Kloos
Text editors
Chris Gordon, Birgitte de Maar
Production
Maarten Kloos, Birgitte de Maar
Translated by
Michael O'Loughlin
Design
Els Kerremans [T & O S M, Rotterdam]
Printing
Industrie, Amsterdam
Publisher
Architectura & Natura Press, Amsterdam,
in conjunction with A R C A M

Frontispiece and cover illustration:
De Nederlanden van 1845

I S B N 90 71570 25 8

Original title: *H.P. Berlage en Amsterdam*
First published by Meulenhoff/Landshoff,
Amsterdam 1987

CONTENTS

CONTENTS

INTRODUCTION

This book was first published (in Dutch) on the occasion of 'De nieuwe werkelijkheid van Berlage', the most significant exhibition yet devoted to the work of the great Dutch architect Hendrik Petrus Berlage. The exhibition, held in 1987, made a considerable impression at the time, particularly because it was held in one of his masterpieces, the Beurs – with which he is best, and sometimes exclusively, associated. This focus, once again, on the Beurs prompted a broader consideration of his contribution to the architecture of Amsterdam however. At the time there was no complete overview of his Amsterdam work in print, and the book therefore filled at least a gap in the literature. But it also did much more.

Presenting an inventory of Berlage's projects within Amsterdam, it includes the smallest alterations; projects realized and unrealized, interesting and less interesting, over-familiar and completely unknown, the well-preserved and the demolished or significantly modified. As a result, it shows all the important facets of Berlage's *œuvre* and contains much material published for the first time. The book is valuable too because, for once, it was not the architectural significance, the urban quality, nor the historical relevance that was the criterion for selection, but the geographical location.

The result is a more down-to-earth image of an architect justifiably famous for his striking creations and his important writings, but who, like every other architect, was also involved in small, more prosaic projects – a simple conversion, a terraced house, a playground. Both Berlage and Amsterdam can thereby be considered from another viewpoint. The architect can be measured against the city, and the city against the architect.

Now, several years after the exhibition, it can be said that appreciation of his work is even greater, evidenced, for instance, by the number of recent publications devoted to Berlage and the growing interest in Berlage among Amsterdam's tourists. At the same time, however, it is sometimes difficult to manage Berlage's heritage. The renovations now necessary to parts of *Plan-Zuid* (whose seventy-fifth anniversary provides an opportune moment for reflection) are proving problematic, the restoration of Mercatorplein and its surroundings is arousing controversy, and the financial costs of operating the Beurs are so high as to threaten its future as a cultural centre.

Only by appreciating Berlage's work can the inspiration be found to tackle these problems in a creative manner and in the spirit of the architect. This book, now accessible to a wider audience, is intended to be our contribution to that appreciation. In producing it ARCAM has incurred many debts, particularly to the Dutch Architectural Institute, custodians of the Berlage archive, which provided most of the illustrations.

MAARTEN KLOOS

BERLAGE AND AMSTERDAM

In the history of architecture, Hendrik Petrus Berlage (1856-1934) and Amsterdam are renowned, at least in the Netherlands. They immediately evoke images: the triple rings of canals with their majestic houses, the creations of Hendrick de Keyser; the former town hall, now Royal Palace, on the Dam, 'the eighth wonder of the world'; and, over two centuries later, the Amsterdam School, the capital's original contribution to modern architecture. Amsterdam is also associated with the Algemeen Uitbreidingsplan (General Extension Plan) of 1935, as a result of which the city developed into the centre of modern town planning.

Berlage is best remembered for the Beurs [project 19], that spare, greyish-red building on Damrak between Central Station and the Royal Palace. Berlage built much more of course, but in retrospect it appears that this creation, completed in 1903, was itself sufficient to ensure his place in architectural history. The extent to which this building contributed to Amsterdam can hardly be underestimated; around the turn of the century, after a long period in the architectural wilderness, Amsterdam once again began to attract the attention of an international circle of architects, critics and architectural historians. That continued too, thanks to the spectacular developments that followed the Beurs around a decade later, developments to which Berlage also contributed with his renowned second extension plan for the south of Amsterdam (1917). With this plan, Berlage created the town-planning framework for the architects of the Amsterdam School, who, in the course of the 1920s, were to make the capital the Mecca of social housing.

Berlage and Amsterdam belong together; they have become inseparable, and the Beurs is the monument that bears constant witness to that unity. Almost thirty years after the Beurs was completed, a relief depicting the architect was added to its façade, and the following text was carved underneath the relief: 'The City Council of Amsterdam has placed this stone in honour of Dr H.P. Berlage, who on 21 February 1926 reached the age of seventy and who built this Beurs in the years 1898-1903.'

Two years later, in 1928, Berlage repaid the compliment in a lecture he gave at the first of the Congrès Internationaux d'Architecture Moderne (CIAM) in La Sarraz, where the international avant-garde in modern architecture were meeting. In this lecture he argued that the Beurs was the result of a harmonious collaboration between the city's administrators, architect and artists, and further that this harmony between politicians, officials and artists was the basis for the subsequent flourishing of Amsterdam's architecture. Looking back, Berlage visualized an uninterrupted period of development from the Beurs to the mature architectural culture of the late 1920s. It had been possible to realize the Beurs, the first major achievement of the modern movement,

*Beurs,
north- and
west façades
[1896-1903]*

because a number of Amsterdam's city councillors were open to the new ideas. Over the years, the city council and the municipal departments became increasingly influenced by these ideas, and ultimately modern architecture was assured of a broad social base. It was not Berlage's intention to portray himself as a pioneer; on the contrary, he wanted to make it clear to his audience that modern architecture had only been able to develop with the support of an enlightened city government that was prepared to accept the new without preconceptions. That he chose Amsterdam as his example naturally reflected his own experience, but, at the same time, it was meant as a tribute to the city whose commissioning the Beurs had ushered in the triumphant rise of the modern movement.

In this interpretation Berlage and Amsterdam were equal partners in the creation of modern architecture in the Netherlands. One city, with a rich architectural heritage, was also the place where modern architecture celebrated its first victories. One man designed a building that anticipated the new culture, marked its starting point and, because it was not an individual creation but a collective product expressing the momentum of the *Zeitgeist* rather than a personal quest, embodied as it were all future architecture. Amsterdam was the cradle of the modern movement and Berlage was the guide who pointed the way to the future. In the 1920s he was able, together with a younger generation of architects, to complete the work begun around 1900 in a continuous and coherent series of designs.

The story outlined here owes as much to imagination, desire and intentions as fact. While it can be supported by numerous sources, it is nevertheless a falsification. As circumstances require, history itself distorts its own past.

Berlage did this, and others (including a number of architectural historians) subsequently went along with him. The present guide, which sets out to do no more than describe Berlage's Amsterdam, is almost bound to show this. There was not the continuity of which Berlage spoke. On the contrary, in terms of the number and scale of the projects, the plans and buildings Berlage designed for Amsterdam are very different; furthermore, Berlage's clients changed considerably over time.

The idea of unity and continuity leads a tenacious existence, not only because it works so well in terms of architectural history, but also because Amsterdam comes off well out of it. The cultural life of the capital was and still is considered to reflect Dutch culture and is advertised as such. Moreover, the tolerant climate of Amsterdam has meant that the city has always been more open to the development of dissident, oppositional or fringe movements. This tradition is a characteristic of Amsterdam, and the city is famous for being able to integrate even the most unusual and controversial into its society without disturbing its social balance. Berlage was a controversial figure and for years the Beurs was the object of criticism. Only in Amsterdam was it possible to realize such a controversial building; indeed, it was even commissioned by the city council. This monument embodies the values, still professed by the city council, of tolerance, progressiveness, resolution and solidarity, and in this way – with all the limitations imposed on architecture of course – it helps to maintain the image of Amsterdam based on these values. Because it is in the cultural capital of the Netherlands, only an Amsterdam building can acquire a national significance completely overshadowing its local and original function. It is therefore not surprising that the city of Amsterdam recommended the Dutch Architectural Institute be housed in the Beurs; and, from an architectural history point of view, no building in the Netherlands would have been more suited to this purpose.

If we survey the series of designs and buildings that Berlage planned and built for Amsterdam, then a picture emerges of a relationship not entirely free of contradictions: the relationship between architect and city council in particular turns out to have been more problematic than was hitherto thought. After an encouraging start in 1881, Berlage worked for many years without any significant successes. Amsterdam provided him with little work. Nevertheless, the architect remained intensely involved with the city, as can be seen from the many designs he made for which he received no commission. Berlage put his heart into Amsterdam, but for the time being the city had no use for him. This somewhat strained relationship only improved in 1896 when, through a series of coincidences, Berlage was commissioned to design the new stock exchange building. This partnership between city and architect, which history suggests was so fruitful and significant, did not last long, and it actually had disastrous consequences for Berlage as an architect. Berlage received no further commissions from the city council between 1900 and 1914 and he spent this period completing existing work. On 1 September 1913, after considerable hesitation and shortly before the political tide began to turn, Berlage joined the firm of Wm.H. Müller & Co. in The Hague and signed an exclusive contract with them for ten years. In 1914 he finally moved to The Hague, where he continued to live in the house he designed for himself on the Violenweg until his death in 1934.

In 1914 the political climate in Amsterdam changed. The Sociaal-Democratische Arbeiders Partij (SDAP, the Social Democratic Labour Party) then had one-third of the seats on the municipal council and F.M. Wibaut became the first socialist alderman in Amsterdam. As a consequence of these political shifts, but for other reasons too, Berlage was asked to revise *Plan-Zuid*, the extension plan he had designed for the south of the city in 1900. And after The Hague, Utrecht and Rotterdam had all shown their high regard for Berlage's architectural and town-planning abilities, Amsterdam too finally offered him more prestigious commissions. In 1926 Berlage was asked to work, together with the Department of Public Works, on a design for a bridge across the Amstel River [53]. It was to be a first-rate work of architecture and town-planning art. The city council rightly named the bridge after Berlage shortly before his death. More honours followed. A debt was thereby repaid, so to speak, and the relationship between Berlage and Amsterdam so completely restored that the impression was created that it had never been troubled.

In compiling material for this guide, several other important issues came to light. Two of them must be briefly discussed here. The first concerns the projects, plans and buildings Berlage designed after 1900. With the exception of his housing and some of his town-planning projects, Berlage's later work has received too little attention. This is true of Dutch architecture in general in the period between the Beurs and the Amsterdam School. Little research has been carried out, and even less published.

The younger generation of architects were either critical or appreciative, but always respectful of the Beurs. The architecture of the decade 1903-13 was comparatively ignored however; it aroused little interest, such was the significance of the Beurs in predicting later designs. Berlage's Beurs potentially already represented these designs and all later movements within Dutch architecture.

Berlage's later work tells a different story though. A great deal must therefore have happened in the years after the completion of the Beurs. Berlage's *œuvre* seems less consistent and lacks the suggestion of purposefulness so characteristic of his designs from the second half of the 1890s. On the one hand, Berlage designed large ideal plans, characterized time and again by academicism and showing the lofty, almost religious significance he ascribed to architecture. On the other hand, Berlage designed stern, rather utilitarian brick buildings, some of whose architectonic quality is only revealed after long consideration. Both the intense ethos and the sometimes dry functionalism make a somewhat exaggerated impression. It is as if Berlage felt the need to resist something.

In 1912 Berlage noted a reaction in the architectural world to his new ideas. He considered this countermovement, which had been gathering force for some time, to be even larger in scale and more dangerous than that which had attempted to impede the birth of the modern movement. He made no secret of his conviction that architecture had been more advanced twenty years before. When Berlage wrote this he was probably thinking of J.A. van Straaten's design sketches for the Bijenkorf, and for the new Effectenbeurs of Jos. Th.J. Cuypers, which was to be built next to his Beurs. In particular, van Straaten's design, with its overstated and therefore irritating references to Jacob van Campen's Town Hall, must have vexed Berlage.

The myth of a continuous development is thus visibly contradicted on Amsterdam's Beursplein. For a better understanding of Berlage's later work, it is more useful therefore to regard it in the context of the struggle then raging among architects than to describe it as the logical progression of what Berlage had achieved around 1900. This struggle climaxed in Berlage's exclusion from the closed competition for the new town hall in Rotterdam. The political decision to exclude him must have deeply offended him and was probably the direct cause of his sharp criticism of the quality of Dutch architecture.

The second of the two points referred to above concerns Berlage's earlier work. While it is true that we are better informed about his earlier work, the compilers of this guide were faced with the problem that Berlage's designs from the 1880s and '90s are not usually judged on their own merits and read in the context of their time but are seen in the light of the later Beurs. A few recent publications apart, little has been written about Berlage's early work as such; most of what has been written tends only to describe to what extent it contributed to the creation of the Beurs. Everything that did not in one way or another pave the way for the Beurs was not considered worth describing.

The unusually multiform of Berlage's early Amsterdam works shows that until around 1892 he drew on a wide variety of styles: Italian and Dutch Renaissance, eclecticism, and a brick rationalism derived from P.J.H. Cuypers. Only in the course of 1893 was Berlage in a position to formulate a consistent theory. In his lecture

'Architecture and Impressionism' (*Bouwkunst en Impressionisme*) he sketched an image of the new architecture he envisaged at the time, and he gave concrete expression to this image of 'impressionistic' architecture in his designs for the De Algemeene insurance company [14], the De Nederlanden van 1845 insurance company [16], and the façade of Raadhuisstraat [18]. In his initial design for the Beurs, however, he did not draw on the impressionistic office architecture he had developed, but once again sought refuge in history. Stylistically and typologically this design echoes Romanesque church architecture. The choir and the tower are proof of this, as are the groin vaults, all of which are supposed to lend the building a sacred or elevated character. Impressionistic architecture was not intended for such monumentality and, according to Berlage, apparently not yet developed enough to create an architectural representation of this character. It is understandable therefore why, even as late as 1896, Berlage drew on a past stylistic period.

Berlage's early work too therefore shows little of the rigid continuity and purposefulness that critics and historians have claimed for it. As far as subject and design are concerned, the early works are also extremely varied. They reveal a versatile architect, erudite and possessing a phenomenal memory for visual images, an architect who followed architectural debates both at home and abroad with great interest and who was well aware too of the cultural and political events of those years. The development of Berlage's work was not linear but occurred in leaps; it did not exclude a step backwards or experiments in a completely different direction.

Berlage's Amsterdam œuvre: a chronology

Berlage's *œuvre* is extremely large. In order to understand it better, it is usual to divide his work into stylistic periods: the period of the historical style, with as its apotheosis the grandiose Monument Historique of 1889, in which all historical styles were incorporated into a single composition; the search for a new style, which culminated in the buildings for De Nederlanden, 1895-96; Berlage's heyday around 1900, when he created the masterpieces that ushered in a new age; and, finally, the long classical period. Such a division needs to be modified in the case of his Amsterdam designs however. As far as the Berlage-Amsterdam relationship is concerned, it is necessary too to take account of Berlage's development in terms of the changing circumstances of his work, and changes in his circle of clients and in the political climate.

1881-89

In 1881 Berlage began his architectural career in Amsterdam with the bureau of Theodor Sanders, who was then working on the construction of the Nederlands Panopticum in Amstelstraat. Sanders was also a board member of the NV Maatschappij voor Volkskoffiehuizen, an association founded in 1879 to provide coffee houses for the working class and for which the bureau built the coffee house De Hoop in 1883-84 [2]. Sanders was a civil engineer and Berlage was one of the best-trained architects of the time; it is therefore not surprising that after 1884 all projects were signed by both Berlage and Sanders, from which it can be concluded that Berlage had become a

*Monument
Historique*
[1889]

Poster for the NHTM [1888]

partner. Furthermore, Sanders' real interest was traffic planning, as a result of which he was forced to give Berlage a free hand in the design of buildings. Sanders saw a great future for the tram and for local and inter-local railway lines connected to the tram network, and the capital was at the centre of his concept.

Sanders' plans and his wealth of ideas certainly encouraged Berlage to concentrate on Amsterdam. He began to realize that the changes brought about by traffic, the new building types, the increase in the scale of architecture, the broader street profiles and so on, could be a threat to the beauty of the city. In his lecture 'Amsterdam and Venice' (1883) he argued that changes should either be carefully carried out so that the picturesque beauty of the city was preserved, or with large-scale interventions to replace the picturesque views with monumental townscapes – as Haussmann had done in Paris. He rejected half-hearted solutions out of hand. The collaboration with Sanders can be seen as Berlage's town-planning apprenticeship. He broadened his knowledge through self-study and design, and by the end of the 1890s Berlage was one of the best-educated and most progressive town planners of his time.

Around the mid-1880s a long period of depression set in in the construction industry; this depression had serious consequences for the bureau of Sanders and Berlage too. Indeed, apart from the sanatorium in Baarn (1887) all the larger commissions had been obtained before 1885. As a result of the building for Focke & Meltzer (1884-86) [4] and the well-regarded competition designs for a new stock exchange in Amsterdam [3], Berlage had already won a certain prestige in professional circles. Subsequent collaboration with Sanders led to few commissions of any significance however: only a little-known design for a large bathhouse on Museumplein (1883), the design for a shopping arcade (1885) [6], an extension to the Munttoren (also 1885) [5], and a shelter and a poster for the Noord-Hollandsche Tramweg Maatschappij (NHTM) (1888) [8]. Though some later work, such as a poster design for the NHTM to mark the opening of a new line to Purmerend (1895), a design for Museumplein (1895-96) [17] and part of the first extension plan for the south of Amsterdam, was related to the railway projects of Sanders, by then, however, Berlage had become independent.

In 1889 the bureau was closed and Berlage had to continue as a free-lance architect, which was exceptionally difficult during this period of economic depression. Fortunately, one client, the firm of De Erven Lucas Bols, remained faithful to Berlage however; from 1887 to 1895 Berlage designed the interiors of several drinking halls for Bols in a number of European cities. Further, from 1887 Berlage was teaching at the Quellijnschool, a school of arts and crafts created in 1879 by P.J.H. Cuypers in Amsterdam. This teaching and the commissions from Bols helped him to maintain a reasonable income despite the difficult times.

The years around 1889 were important for a number of reasons, though their significance would only later become clear. Through his marriage, Berlage had come into contact with L. Bienfait, the co-director of the Proefstation voor Bouwmaterialen Koning & Bienfait (a building materials research laboratory). This institute was first located in the railway office building at the Droogbak, but in 1900 it moved to commercial premises designed by Berlage on Da Costakade [22]. Berlage was also related to some of the Tachtigers (a leading Dutch artistic movement of the period): the sister of Berlage's wife later married the brother of the famous poet Albert Verwey, who in turn was the brother-in-law of Frederik van Eeden, himself a poet and also a psychologist and utopian philosopher. Berlage's lengthy friendship with Albert Verwey naturally had deeper origins, but these family connections must have contributed to the fact that Berlage was asked to design houses for van Eeden in Bussum (1892) and for the mother-in-law of Albert Verwey in Noordwijk (1896).

Berlage, his brother-in-law L. Bienfait, and Theodor Sanders were apparently politically committed; at the beginning of 1888 they signed a pamphlet calling for the formal establishment of the radical electoral association Amsterdam, a political grouping that had then just split from the liberals. The radicals originally also gave political shelter to the socialists, but the radicals' leader, M.W.F. Treub, soon outlined a new course for the radicals in between the socialists and the liberals. Berlage was even invited to be a candidate for the radicals in the city council elections of 1891, but, for reasons that remain unclear, he refused. Between 1885 and 1891 the so-called Breero Club, a society of intellectuals, politicians and artists, acted as a spawning ground for radical ideas. Through this club Berlage had met, among others, E.D. Pijzel, P.L. Tak, who was later to be a prominent socialist, and the radical Treub. In 1892 Pijzel invited Berlage to design a house for him on Van Baerlestraat [13]. Tak later became editor of the famous weekly *De Kroniek*, the first issue of which appeared on 1 January 1895. Berlage was a regular contributor to the architecture section and, particularly in the first two years, he wrote many articles.

Residence for Frederik van Eeden, Bussum [1892-93]

Volkshuis, Lochem [1891-92]

He also got to know several other contributors, the so-called Negentigers. It was through Tak that Berlage came into contact with Henri Polak, the chairman of the Algemeene Nederlandsche Diamantbewerkersbond (ANDB, the Diamond Workers' Union), and probably also with Wibaut. The acquaintance with Polak ultimately led to the commission to design the headquarters of the ANDB [20]. Treub also chose Berlage as the architect for the new stock exchange building, after Berlage had gained a reputation as the most radical architect of his time.

1889-96

Berlage began his free-lance career by participating in a number of competitions. These brought him little success and few commissions however. In 1890 a cousin arranged for him to be asked to redesign the offices of the firm of Kerkhoven & Co. [9]. Prior to 1892 he had only designed a few houses, realized some interiors for the firm of Bols, and built the Volkshuis (community centre) in Lochem, the commission for which he also probably got through a cousin. Neither the number nor the size of the commissions was impressive. Apart from the plain buildings he built and whose sobriety probably reflects budgetary considerations, Berlage gained a reputation as a very skilful draughtsman and designer of fantastic projects, such as the new façade for the cathedral in Milan (1887), the Monument Historique (1889) and a fantastic architectural sketch (1892), probably intended as a design for the façade of a royal palace [11].

A dramatic change in Berlage's fortunes occurred in 1893. In that year Berlage drew up the definitive plans for the building of De Algemeene, and, in addition to other things, he was working on the manuscript for his lecture 'Architecture and Impressionism'. The building was to make Berlage famous; the lecture, on the other hand, would make him notorious. For Berlage the offices of De Algemeene were not only his first major commission, they also represented a breakthrough in his practice as architect; whereas Sanders and he together had failed to gain access to Amsterdam high finance, Berlage on his own had succeeded. Berlage acted as an expert adviser for De Algemeene and carried out many commissions, including two large ones: the building of De Algemeene's German head office in Leipzig (1902) and the colossal extension to the building on Damrak (1902-05). He was also commissioned by the company to design its offices in Surabaya (then part of the Dutch East Indies) (1900) and housing and shops along Hobbemastraat (1904) [30]. It is likely too that the design of two blocks of houses on Museumplein was related to the company's investment activities. Everything about De Algemeene was unusual, and mostly spectacular: the first building, the enormous growth of the company, the colossal extension, the company's catastrophic bankruptcy at the beginning of the 1920s, and the spectacular fire of 1963, which completely destroyed the building.

In November 1893, shortly before the building's completion, Berlage gave his lecture 'Architecture and Impressionism'. The lecture had an astonishing effect. Architects felt especially aggrieved because Berlage had completely rejected what they understood by architecture. Berlage argued that architecture was under threat from all sides. Fantasy was being compromised by growing bureaucracy and increasingly strict building regulations. The quality of design and execution was threatened because the architect was no longer granted the time to work conscientiously. Finally, the value of architecture was being denied since insufficient funds were available to enable architects to design buildings whose materials, structure and aesthetics could be considered satisfactory enough for them to be regarded as architecture. According to Berlage, this frugality arose from the financial considerations of clients who, when estimating costs, failed to regard a building of high architectural quality as any more significant than a hovel with a decorated façade. The lack of money, Berlage suggested, was also a consequence of new social and political ideas. The time for palaces and expensive programmes of decoration was past: instead housing, schools, buildings to provide social amenities, and, by no means least, completely new cities must be built. All this had to be done cheaply because the large scale of these developments could only be realized if money was not wasted. Berlage, however, wanted to maintain the structural and aesthetic quality of architecture, and even improve it, because for him the professional code of the architect was unassailable. He was prepared though to abandon the entire decorative mishmash of valuable materials and ornaments. Instead of these, he proposed an 'impressionistic' architecture, one that would appeal to the viewer through mass, relief, silhouette and extremely economically applied sculpture alone.

In his lecture Berlage accepted the reality as it then was. He felt that growing social awareness and democratic principles were positive forces in society. On the other hand, he was also sympathetic to the position of major clients, who regarded architecture primarily as investment. Moreover, Berlage made an architectural virtue of the necessity of bureaucracy, building regulations and the lack of time and money – and that is precisely what offended his colleagues; he was stripping architecture of everything that was precious to them. Impressionistic architecture steered a *via media* between the interests of capital and labour, and there, somewhere in the middle, were the radicals, led by Treub. Berlage had made an architectural translation, so to speak, of their electoral programme. This is why Treub, elected Alderman for Public Works in Amsterdam in 1895, chose Berlage when he had to propose an architect for the new stock exchange. It was only Berlage whom he could rely on to design a building that would continuously bear witness to radical reformist ideas.

This development in Berlage's career could not have been foreseen at the time of his 1893 lecture. In that year, the same year Treub had been elected Alderman for Finance and had embarked on a series of radical reforms, Berlage was, among other things, developing a symbol for the city of Amsterdam; not a heraldic symbol, but an architectural one – on stage. Collaborating with Leo Simons, who later became the director of the Wereldbibliotheek publishing company, he worked on a new staging of Vondel's *Gijsbreght van Aemstel*. Like so many of Berlage's plans, this project had an interesting history. In 1889 Leo Simons asked Berlage if he would like to design a theatre, probably intended for the recently founded Toneelvereeniging. Berlage later said that for him, an architect who had just turned free-lance, this was a wonderful opportunity and an unusually attractive commission. No drawings of the design have survived; perhaps none were ever made, because on the night of 19

February 1890 the wooden theatre on Leidseplein was completely burnt out and the credit extended to Simons by a banker friend was recalled in order to finance the reconstruction of this theatre. Berlage continued to work on Simon's project, however, and he designed a small theatre which was supposed to be built on the site of a former gasworks close to what is now Frederiksplein. These plans have also been lost, and the theatre was never built. This setback marked the beginning of a long friendship though. In 1900 Simons commissioned Berlage to build him a house, Villa Parkwyck – 'the house with the handle' – on Van Eeghenstraat [24]. When Simons moved to The Hague in 1913 Berlage built a villa for him on Prinsevinkenpark. Simons probably also introduced him to the housing association Ons Huis, an association with which Simons, concerned to improve the social welfare of the working classes, was closely involved. In 1904 Berlage was commissioned by Ons Huis to renovate and extend the association's building, which had been designed by C.B. Posthumus Meyjes sen. [29].

Simons and Berlage were apparently not discouraged by the failure of their theatre plans because in 1890 Simons wrote to the publisher Erven F. Bohn that he and Berlage had developed an idea for a fine edition of Vondel's *Gijsbreght van Aemstel*. The beautiful folio edition appeared in the course of the 1890s. Berlage's task was to design the stage décors. This presented a number of difficulties, however, since theatre was then in a state of flux and new ideas were rapidly succeeding each other. After many experiments, Berlage and Simons found a solution that not only represented a successful attempt to reform Amsterdam theatre, but also implied a new interpretation of Vondel's *Gijsbreght*. The theme of the play,

Stage décor for Gijsbreght van Aemstel [1893]

Simons claimed in his introduction, and Berlage in a lecture on theatre design, is the destruction of Amsterdam. Whatever happens inside or outside the city, Amsterdam remains the main figure in the tableau presented by Vondel. As a symbol of this, Berlage designed a city gate with part of a city wall remaining visible throughout the entire performance. It was old Dutch in form and, as Berlage expressed it, stately and awe-inspiring. He chose the medieval Sint-Antoniespoort on the Nieuwmarkt as his model.

The required historical setting of the décor notwithstanding, Berlage succeeded in his experiments with the illustrations for *Gijsbreght* in finding an architectural form that immediately evoked an association with Amsterdam in the minds of theatre-goers. In the following years, Berlage was to increasingly liberate forms from their historical ballast. It is only the details of the staircase tower and the buttress of the building for De Nederlanden on Muntplein, for example, that echo the original medieval Regulierspoort, which had been partly demolished by Hendrick de Keyser at the beginning of the seventeenth century and converted into the Munttoren. The south façade of the Beurs broadly repeats, without any stylistic references, the silhouette of the old Town Hall on the Dam, which was replaced in the seventeenth century by that of van Campen. The form of de Keyser's building is widely known because of an often-copied painting by Pieter Saenredam and numerous engravings. In the *Gijsbreght* illustrations we find the origins of Berlage's quest for a national formal language, which clearly indicates its roots in the capital. It is not for nothing that the plan of the façade of De Nederlanden, which adorns the cover of this book, displays the arms of both Amsterdam and the Netherlands. Its significance is ambiguous: here Berlage is underlining, perhaps unnecessarily, the fact that he had designed the Amsterdam headquarters of an insurance company called De Nederlanden; but, at the same time, the juxtaposition of the two coats of arms expresses the hope that this Amsterdam building will mark the beginning of a new Dutch architecture, the beginning of a contemporary, modern form of the old Dutch architecture, one that would bear witness to the revival and flourishing of Amsterdam after a long period of stagnation and slow growth. It was only with the Beurs, however, that the idea Berlage developed during work on décors for *Gijsbreght*, that of creating a permanent symbol for Amsterdam, would actually be realized.

After Berlage had completed the building for De Algemeene, he was awarded two other major commissions. In 1895-96 he built a head office in The Hague and a branch office in Amsterdam for De Nederlanden. This company was to remain Berlage's most faithful client. In 1901, 1909 and 1911 he drew up plans for the alteration and extension of both buildings and designed new offices in Rotterdam (1910), Nijmegen (1911), Batavia (1913) and the company's new head office in The Hague (1920, realized 1927). As well as this, the director of De Nederlanden, Carel Henny, gave Berlage many private commissions.

The building for De Nederlanden demonstrates even more consistently than its immediate predecessor, the offices for De Algemeene, the aesthetic principle of impressionistic architecture. Berlage had described the effect of an impressionistic building: 'There it stands, a greyish-red outline, with its large wall surface, darker above, and an angular, simple and beautiful profile against the sky: a splendid background, natural in appearance, thousand-coloured but still against the colourful bustle of the street.' In order to formulate his theory of impressionistic architecture, Berlage had to dispose of architectural tradition, which had become suffocated by considerations of historical style, and not everyone supported him. Nevertheless, Berlage's fame as the most modern and most radical architect was definitely established by 1895. The criticism, which had been unanimously positive and often even enthusiastic in the case of the building for De Algemeene, took a new turn however: Berlage was accused of importing American ideas and his architecture disqualified as shabby and offering little more than 'walls with holes'. But at that time, office buildings were still regarded by many as utility buildings, and a greater degree of freedom was permitted in their design than in the case of monumental buildings like museums, stations, town halls, etc. What is remarkable is that most architects failed to take advantage of this freedom but tried to find design solutions by drawing on plans more appropriate to palaces. Berlage was the first to take full advantage of this freedom. In the case of De Nederlanden, hostile criticism remained swamped under the broad public approval that met his ideas. A real storm of protest was unleashed only after Berlage had published his plans for the Beurs, when it was clear that he had also approached this monument according to his ideas of impressionistic architecture.

1896-1900

The building for De Nederlanden was not yet finished when in the autumn of 1895 Treub asked Berlage if he would be prepared to design the new stock exchange building. By April of that year the appearance of the building had already been publicized. As with the De Algemeene, Berlage had exhibited a fine drawing of the façade proposed. The exhibition received considerable attention. In *De Kroniek* of 21 April 1895 J.E. van der Pek, a friend and kindred spirit of Berlage, wrote a wildly enthusiastic article about the design: 'It appears to me that the building for "de Nederlanden" will become a new expression of Berlage's conviction in his art; that is reason enough for contentment, but the fact that this re-building necessitates the demolition of a four-year-old work of pretentious sham art is yet a further reason why our contentment should instill in us a genuine happiness. A work of sham art less, and most probably one work of architecture more! The Amsterdammers can truly count themselves lucky.'

Van der Pek's article probably also expressed the reasons behind Treub's decision to entrust Berlage with the building of the Beurs. At that time, Berlage was the only architect capable of expressing in architectural terms the innovative changes introduced by the radicals into Amsterdam municipal politics. In addition, impressionistic architecture, the art of frugality, was suitable because the budget for the Beurs was actually quite minimal. If we survey the monuments constructed in the nineteenth and twentieth centuries, the Beurs is probably the cheapest of its type. The Beurs was also an expression of the shared political ideas of Treub and Berlage however. As an old radical, Berlage was sympathetic to more or less the same social ideas as Treub, and the alderman could therefore expect the architect would loyally co-operate on this enterprise, which – as would be apparent shortly after – would become the final chapter in radical municipal politics.

In addition to these considerations, the difficult relationship between Treub and the city architect, A.W. Weissman, also played a role. After several major conflicts, Weissman was forced to resign. There was therefore no point in Treub looking for an architect in the circles frequented by this conservative and influential figure. Furthermore, there were few architects who sympathized with Treub's ideas. The progressives, like K.P.C. de Bazel, W. Kromhout, van der Pek, W.C. Bauer and others, had no record of service at the time, and it would have been difficult to recommend any one of them to the Beurs committee. In short, if he wanted to avoid delays through petitions, protests and other forms of opposition, Berlage was Treub's only possible choice.

In 1896, after Weissman's resignation, Berlage became *de facto* the new city architect. Unfortunately, in November of that year Treub had ceased to be a member of the city government, and gradually the capital's administration began to run out of steam: the council quickly regressed into the bourgeois, somewhat complacent state that had characterized it before the rise of the radicals at the beginning of the 1890s. Initially, Berlage noticed little of this because, in 1897, his design for the façade of a house and shop on Raadhuisstraat [18] was accepted by the city council as an example of the type of future development it hoped for. This decision must have made Berlage optimistic about the capital's architectural development.

Furthermore, in December 1897 Berlage was approached by Henri Polak with a request to design a new building for the ANDB. This created an unusual situation.

On the one hand, Berlage was building for the capital and a city council that was coming to regard with increasing disfavour the vigour of the trade union movement, and, on the other hand, he was to build the headquarters of the strongest and most progressive trade union in the Netherlands, whose members formed the core of the Sociaal-Democratische Arbeiders Partij (SDAP, the Social Democratic Labour Party).

It was not until 1899 that Berlage found a solution to this problem. He designed a double monument. In the Plantage neighbourhood he erected a Volkshuis, which looked like a fortress on the outside but a palace inside. In this building, the symbol of organized labour, the society of the future and a new culture based on democratic principles would be planned. On Damrak, on the other hand, Berlage designed a symbolic town hall that reflected the unity and harmony of this future social order; it has a tribunal (the vestibule), in which judgment on the class society of that time was pronounced, a civic hall (the commodities exchange), which could also be used for festive occasions, and a majestic reception room for the city government (the hall of the Chamber of Commerce). This spatial trio was inspired by the Town Hall of van Campen, but also by the Rijksmuseum of P.J.H. Cuypers. Even the collaboration of architect and poet has historical antecedents: for Berlage and Verwey, but also for Cuypers and J.A. Alberdingk Thijm, van Campen and Vondel were the model. We see here thus another attempt to revive the Golden Age.

While Berlage was working out his ideas for the Beurs and the ANDB building, he was asked by the city council to act as aesthetic advisor on the design for a new Amstel bridge drawn up by the Department of Public Works

[28]. Seventeen years earlier, Sanders had published a fantastic design for a bridge with a belvedere on exactly the same site – an old dream would therefore be realized. In March 1900 Berlage was invited by the city council to design an extension plan for the south of Amsterdam. This gave him the opportunity to invent a structure in which existing buildings and ones yet to be designed by him could be brought into a spatial relationship with each other. Berlage was eager to accept the commission, and, despite already having many other commissions, he managed to complete work on *Plan-Zuid* within seven months. The complacency within the city government led to the plan laying in a drawer gathering dust for four years, however, and it was not until October 1904 that the extension plan was discussed by the council; it was approved a few months later.

1901-13

The year 1901 was of decisive importance in Berlage's career. In March of that year the mayor of Amsterdam, S.A. Vening Meinesz, a supporter of the radicals, announced he was stepping down. He was succeeded by the conservative alderman F.W. van Leeuwen. The ten years during which Vening Meinesz had held office had been unusually significant, Tak wrote on his departure. 'One by one the large utilities have come under the control of the municipality, whose management during the period of his visionary leadership has undergone a real revolution. And whoever attended the Council towards the end of Treub's period as alderman will have retained a memory of the way in which the mayor supported his younger and vigorous assistant, generously and without reservation.' For Berlage too it marked the end of an especially important few years. The city council lost many of its most able members, and consequently its administrative strength was weakened. A number of capable councillors, including a radical, resigned, and, as a result of an electoral pact whose purpose was to re-elect outgoing councillors and to exclude the SDAP, new and progressive candidates had no chance of being elected in the municipal elections of 1901. This pact was successful, and though the SDAP had considerable influence outside Amsterdam, it was 1902 before the first socialist (Henri Polak) was elected to the council.

For Berlage, these developments must have been very disappointing, all the more so since he was denied any further commissions by the new conservative administration. His vision of the Amsterdam of the future, which he had visualized in his many designs, buildings, and also in *Plan-Zuid*, was shattered. Less significant, but nevertheless symptomatic of the altered relations, was the petty refusal of the city government to co-operate on an illustrated publication about the Beurs. Berlage had had this idea for a long time. He had wanted something equal in quality to the *Gijsbreght van Aemstel* portfolio or the fine edition on the Rijksmuseum, and, considering the importance of the Beurs and its relationship to the Rijksmuseum, it was a reasonable expectation. The plan came to nothing however. Only the lithographs of the beautiful drawings by H.J.M. Walenkamp in *De Architect* (1901) give some impression of the nature of the proposed publication.

Until 1905 Berlage's bureau was fairly active; after that, however, things became more difficult, not only because of the economic crisis of 1907, but also because of

Berlage's image as an architect with leftist sympathies. While it is true Berlage sympathized with the labour movement, he was no socialist. It was, however, thanks to the solidarity of the socialists that Berlage survived these difficult years and later became once again much in demand. In 1906, probably through his old friend Henri Polak, for whom he had designed a house in Laren the year before, he was commissioned to design a building for the Arbeiders Coöperatie Voorwaarts (a workers' association) in Rotterdam. Furthermore, in 1907 he was more or less imposed by the board of the ANDB on the Arbeiders Coöperatie De Dageraad to revise the façades of a building in Amsterdam designed by J.W.F. Hartkamp [35].

It was not until 1910 that Berlage's fortunes changed much for the better. In that year the housing associations Algemeene Woningbouwvereniging (AWV) and De Arbeiderswoning were founded. Most of their members and board members were also members of the SDAP and the trade union movement. Furthermore, many diamond workers were also members of the AWV. Berlage became the AWV's first architect and J.C. van Epen, who had already submitted plans for social housing to the board of the ANDB, became his assistant. De Arbeiderswoning also chose Berlage as architect, but de Bazel, who designed a great number of dwellings on Van Beuningenplein, was also employed. With his blocks of housing for Tolstraat [40], in the Transvaal neighbourhood [41], the Indische and Staatslieden neighbourhoods [44 and 43], and finally in Amsterdam-Noord [42], Berlage ended his Amsterdam period in a blaze of glory. He was now, despite lack of support from the city government, also a great pioneer in the field of housing.

*Arbeiders
Coöperatie
Voorwaarts,
Rotterdam
[1906]*

Extension plan for the Transvaal neighbourhood [1916-19]

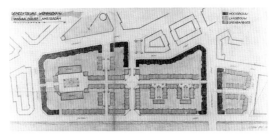

Extension plan for south Amsterdam [1900]

Second extension plan for south Amsterdam [1917]

Nonetheless, given the relatively unfavourable circumstances in the capital, Berlage began to look beyond Amsterdam for work as early as 1907, and he increasingly turned his attention to The Hague. With the help of friends, but above all because his *Plan-Zuid* had secured his reputation as an extremely able town planner, in April 1907 Berlage was invited to design a new extension plan for The Hague in collaboration with the Director of Public Works. The resulting plan was published in 1909 and incorporated many new insights into the field of town planning. With it, Berlage definitively established his reputation as the leading town planner of his day. In the years that followed, Berlage's activities became increasingly concentrated in The Hague and in 1914, now under contract to Wm.H. Müller & Co., he moved there.

1914 and after

In 1914 Wibaut, a socialist, became Alderman for Public Housing in Amsterdam, and just a year later the city government launched the 3500 dwellings plan. There was a considerable shortage of housing at the time, the number of slum dwellings was increasing, and the housing associations were unable to meet the demand for good cheap dwellings. The municipality therefore decided to build houses itself. The Housing Department approached the best and most experienced architects of the time and eventually chose de Bazel, van der Pek and Berlage. Their decision led to uproar in the council chamber, however, since neither Berlage nor de Bazel lived in Amsterdam. Wibaut and the Director of the Housing Department, A. Keppler, nevertheless succeeded in defending their choice and Berlage was commissioned to design an entire district in the Transvaal neighbourhood. The irony of the story is that Berlage was in fact contractually bound to the firm of Wm.H. Müller & Co. and this prevented him from taking on additional design work. Town planning was permitted under this contract, however, and so Berlage was free to design the urban plan. He formed a company with the bureau Gratama & Versteeg, which was responsible for the design and execution of the architectural plans.

Apart from the powerful support of Wibaut, that Berlage was able to obtain this commission also had something to do perhaps with another event. The 1902 Housing Act decreed that municipal extension plans had to be revised every ten years, and in January 1915 the first *Plan-Zuid* would come up for revision. The Director of Public Works, A.W. Bos, therefore wrote a letter to Berlage in January 1914 offering to discuss any prospective changes. Berlage apparently agreed, and in October of the same year he was commissioned to redraft his own *Plan-Zuid*. Berlage drew up a completely new plan, one unmatched in the Netherlands for its impact on the urban development of a city. Since then Berlage has become a legend, and Amsterdam has done everything to foster this legend.

MANFRED BOCK

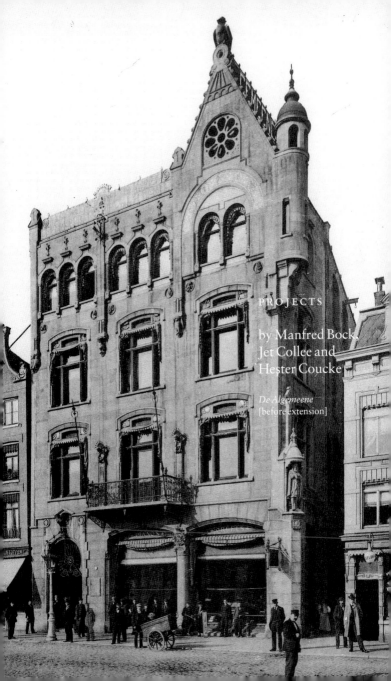

by Manfred Bock,
Jet Collee and
Hester Coucke

De Algemeene
[before extension]

Fountain *c.* 1883
Vondelpark
Not realized

Berlage made two variations on a design for a fountain intended for the pavilion (now the filmmuseum) in the Vondelpark. From the additional site plans it is clear they were not designed for the same spot. In the first design the fountain is placed in the middle of the water; in the second it is on the bank diagonally opposite the pavilion. Both variations are in a neo-Renaissance style and have a characteristic pyramid construction.

The fountains consist of two parts: a basin and a dish on a base. The dish is placed in the middle of the basin and forms the actual fountain. The water collects in the basin. The structure of the dish is largely the same in both designs, but the first has a noticeably more exuberant line and richer decoration. Both are decorated with motifs derived from the flora and fauna that live in the water. The overflow-pipes, for example, are in the form of water monsters, and the dish in the first design is constructed out of four shells. The basins differ in form however. Through its position in the water, the basin in the first design has a characteristic round form, so that the fountain appears to emerge out of the water. In the second design this round form is replaced by broad steps, which adapt easily to the slope of the bank. The platform and steps are closed on the bank side, and the water of the fountain thereby flows by itself along the steps and into the pond. Both basins are decorated with the same motifs as the dish. In the first the steps that descend slanted to the water are decorated with frogs; in the second they are decorated with dolphins and turtles.

First design

Second design

Volkskoffiehuis De Hoop 1883-84
75 De Ruyterkade
Function: coffee house, lodging house and restaurant
With: Th. Sanders
Commissioned by: Maatschappij voor Volkskoffiehuizen
Demolished

Berlage and Sanders both put their names to the design for this coffee house and it was their first joint project after Berlage had gone to work for Sanders at the end of 1881. It is not surprising that Sanders won this commission: he was a board member of the Maatschappij voor Volkskoffiehuizen, founded in 1879. The building was demolished shortly after 1920 to make way for an extension to Central Station. The façade is constructed from the bottom up, with a basement, a raised ground floor, two middle floors, a top floor and an attic. A similar layout is to be found in the building for Focke & Meltzer (1885) [4], also designed by Berlage and Sanders. The floors are marked off from each other by a horizontal articulation. A moulding has been placed between the raised ground floor and the middle floor, as well as between the two middle floors, for example.

The façade is divided vertically into two. The left side is set back somewhat with respect to the right, where the entrance is located. The effect of this projection is reinforced towards the top of the building and culminates in a crowning gable, which leans sharply forward. This striking motif is supported by corbels and pilasters. The design of the gable was inspired by seventeenth-century Dutch examples and can also be seen in Haarlem's town hall. The ground floor and the two middle floors are vertically articulated with round arches, with a distinction

being made between the two parts of the façade by the use of broader arches below the top of the façade. The arches enclose the windows and the entrance. The top floor is simple in design. There are four windows over the entire width, in line with those underneath. The window on the right is bordered and divided by mullions in the form of pilasters; these serve to support the corbels above. A similar form is used for the central mullions of the three windows on the left. Although these support the roof, their form is more determined by aesthetic considerations.

The decorations, as well as the style, of the architectural articulation are derived from the Dutch Renaissance. The shell ornaments, the scrollwork, the pilasters and the curved pediment on the gable are all inspired by this style, as are the triangular pediments and the pilasters with Corinthian capitals for the windows of the first middle floor. The entire front is built in red brick. Stone is used for the horizontal mouldings, the decorations, the pediments, the capitals and the relieving arches.

Stock Exchange Building 1884-85
Damrak
With: Th. Sanders
Competition entry, *not realized*

The repeatedly altered and adapted Beurs by J.D. Zocher was the subject of complaints from the day of its opening in 1848. In 1879 the mayor and aldermen of Amsterdam invited designs for a new stock exchange building. Over the years numerous projects were submitted and many sites proposed. The council finally decided to designate Damrak, which was subsequently partially filled in in 1883, as the site for the new building. A year later an international competition for the new exchange building was announced. Five teams of architects were invited to participate in the final round, held in 1885. The 'Mercaturae' design by Sanders and Berlage won third prize, the first and second prizes going to L.M. Cordonnier and the team of J. Groll and F. Ohmann respectively.

The definitive version of 'Mercaturae' does not differ much in appearance from the first design. The silhouette with high towers is Old Dutch picturesque. The authentic character is confirmed by the brick and stone construction, and references like those to the tower of Hendrick de Keyser's Beurs or the gable of the town hall in The Hague, and by designing the crown of the tower in the style of the Franeker town hall. The interior has undergone the greatest change. Instead of the cinquecento decoration, which radiates the same atmosphere as their design for a vestibule for a royal palace [7], there are walls of clean masonry with stone bands. The iron roof structure with tie rods was left visible.

Beurs,
second design
[1885]

Focke & Meltzer 1884-86
152 Kalverstraat
Function: shop with offices
With: Th. Sanders
Commissioned by: Focke & Meltzer

The architects took full advantage of the favourable position of this site. The building is striking for its dimensions, which were more imposing then than they are now; its style, derived from the Venetian Renaissance; the corner tower; and the plate-glass windows, whose size was considered enormous at that time.

Despite the difference in width, Berlage treated both façades equally. The façade on Spui is one bay wider; a narrower bay with a deviating articulation has been added. Originally, a deep balcony was placed on the first floor of the façade on Spui. The balustrade was in the building line of the adjacent building. In a later alteration this balcony was reduced to a barely projecting parapet. The façades are enclosed in rusticated lesenes and divided horizontally in three: above the ground floor there are two upper floors, slightly recessed, separated by a moulding and finished with a powerfully profiled cornice jutting out from the façade. Above, there is a recessed top floor lower in height than the two middle floors. The attic floor is not in a neo-Renaissance style but in that of the French Second Empire. The vertical articulation of the façades is derived conventionally from the classical orders: the free-standing granite columns with Doric bronze capitals bear double Ionic pilasters on the first floor and double Corinthian pilasters on the second.

The corner has been treated as a tower. Above the monumental entrance to the shop, the oriel windows project

and are supported by powerful but finely sculpted corbels. The tower is crowned by a round tempietto covered
with a green domed roof. The form of the windows on the
two middle floors is derived from the quattrocento. The
double-arched window is spanned by a single arch and
decorated with a medallion. The illustrations on the med-
allions refer to the client, the firm of Focke & Meltzer,
which dealt in glasswork, pottery and porcelain. On the
first floor, for example, there are portraits of artists –
Pallissy, Luca della Robbia, Wedgwood and the Crabeth
brothers – engaged in the faience and glass industries.
The corbels on which the bay windows rest are decorated
with vases, tendrils, leaves and cherub heads. The frieze
above the entrance bore the name of the company originally housed here.

The attic floor on the Spui side has large studio windows. A photographic studio was housed here. The central windows were originally doors giving access on to a
balcony. From early drawings it is clear that this studio
was not a part of the original programme. Old photo-
graphs show that it was added soon after.

Annexe to the Munttoren 1885
Muntplein (formerly Sophiaplein)
Not realized

At the end of May 1885 the old annexe to the Munttoren
was demolished and the city of Amsterdam commissioned a committee of architects, assembled especially for
the purpose, to design a new one. On the basis of this
committee's design, Berlage made four studies of his own;
perspective views of two of these were made.

Berlage's considerations were twofold: on the one
hand, he was interested in a balanced architectural relationship between a monument and a new building, and,
on the other hand, he was also interested in the impact of
the ensemble on the appearance of the city. In the committee's design the tower and the annexe are merged into
one architectural unit, so that the tower loses its independence and the whole construction gives the impression of being a small church. Berlage, however, preserves
the independence of the tower. He achieves this by linking
the annexe to the tower only in the type of mater-ials
used, the masonry, and by giving the roof of the annexe
an independent form and silhouette. Only in the horizontal articulation of the wall surface is the annexe in
harmony with the divisions of the tower's façade. The
profile of the tower's base, for example, is continued in
the annexe, and the roof edge of the latter echoes the cor-
responding horizontal articulation of the tower. Though
never realized, Berlage's designs attracted the attention of
the Maatschappij tot Bevordering der Bouwkunst (a society for the promotion of architecture), which awarded
him a silver medal for the best designs for an unbuilt
work.

*One of
the two
perspective
drawings*

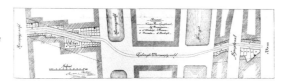

Arcade: plan

Arcade between the Dam and Westermarkt 1885
(now Paleisstraat, Raadhuisstraat)
Function: shopping arcade and tramway
With: Th. Sanders
Not realized

When Berlage came to work at Sanders' bureau in 1881,
Sanders was busy developing a new network of tramlines
for Amsterdam and its environs. An element in his plans
was a connecting route between the Dam and Rozengracht. Sanders published the first plan for what would
later be called Raadhuisstraat in 1883. Two years later he
published a second design; unlike the first, this also bore
Berlage's name. In contrast to the monumental plan of
1883 and the ultimately realized Raadhuisstraat, the altered design has a provisional character. The tramway
followed a route that minimized the number of buildings
that would have to be demolished. The architectural articulation of the arcade concept is restrained. It was only
on Nieuwezijds Voorburgwal, along the axis of the Royal
Palace, that the architects chose a monumental arch.

Vestibule for a Royal Palace 1885
Not realized

In April 1885 the association Architectura et Amicitia announced an open competition for a royal palace in the country's capital. It was intended to stimulate solutions to an old problem, one created by Louis Napoleon's occupation of the Town Hall on the Dam. Since then, the building has been called a palace, and the seat of local government has had to be located elsewhere in the city, to the considerable dissatisfaction of many people. Berlage probably toyed with the idea of entering this competition, but his efforts resulted ultimately only in a fantastic sketch of the interior of a vestibule. The perspective shows much affinity with the first competition entry for the Beurs, dating from the previous year. Both designs were inspired by the Caracalla baths in Rome.

Tram shelter for the NHTM 1888
Stationsplein
Function: waiting room and office at the terminus of the NHTM's
Amsterdam-Edam line
With: Th. Sanders
Commissioned by: Noord-Hollandsche Tramweg Maatschappij
(NHTM)
Demolished

The purpose and floor-plan of this building were simple: a 6 × 4.5 metre waiting room for the public and an office measuring 2 × 3 metres. The waiting room was intended for passengers going by boat across the IJ to the actual terminus of the tram line. Berlage and Sanders, who was then director of the NHTM, believed that the terminus of a tram line in a major city had to look elegant and offer passengers sufficient comfort. The roof, the most striking aspect of the building, expressed the function of a tram shelter, which is in fact nothing more than that of a sheltered spot. The woodwork is richly treated, as is the zinc and ironwork of the roof covering. By using various materials, such as plain American pine for the structure, coloured and glazed bricks for the footing, and coloured glass and faience tiles, it becomes a colourful whole. As far as form is concerned, the building bears no similarity to Berlage's later work, but in terms of material and therefore colour it does. Berlage would always continue to use glazed bricks and faience tiles in his designs.

Kerkhoven & Co. 1889-90
115 Herengracht
Function: office building
Commissioned by: Kerkhoven & Co.

The spatial layout of this building can be read from the division of the façade across the four floors. The window arrangement of the bottom two floors shows that there is a difference between the floor levels of the left and right sides of the building. In the left part there is a basement and a raised ground floor; in the right the entrance at street level is combined with a low first floor. The top-two-floor windows indicate that here the floors are at the same level. With the help of continuous horizontal bands of stone placed at the lintels, transoms, and sills of the windows the façade is formed into a single whole. Striking here is the treatment of the basement. It consists of a substantial plinth, topped by a slanting stone moulding that meanders around the windows and continues past the entrance. The profiled projection of the stepped gable seems to repeat this motif. Under the projection is a stone tablet with the year, painted white; this continues the roof edge of the left part of the building. The unity of the façade is also guaranteed by the use of stone for the keystones and imposts above the windows. The stone frame around the entrance, the decorations on the tympani under the relieving arches above the large windows on the ground floor, and the stepped gable are all motifs derived from the formal language of the Dutch Renaissance. Unlike the interior, the façade has not been altered since it was originally built.

Drawing of façade

Façade of a house 1891
17 Egelantiersgracht

Only the façade of this house was designed by Berlage. The façade, still in its original state, is composed of heterogeneous elements and can therefore be described as eclectic. The lower part, with its vigorous rustication, is typical of the German-Dutch neo-Renaissance. Above the ground floor there is a façade that echoes P.J.H. Cuypers' Rijksmuseum, particularly in the way the horizontal is articulated by bands of stone at the lintels, transoms and sills of the windows, in the profiled relieving arches with the tympani filled with ornamentation, and the way in which the jambs of the windows are profiled. These motifs and the floors, continuously projecting forward on consoles, have their inspiration in the housing architecture of the early Renaissance, which was then still dominated by the medieval tradition. On the other hand, the rather exuberant outline of the gable, decorated with scrollwork, spheres and a segmental pediment, is reminiscent of Dutch mannerism from around 1600.

An unbuilt variation of this façade shows that Berlage also studied examples from the first half of the sixteenth century. This can be seen in the basket-arch-shaped niche, the equally basket-arch-shaped relieving arches, and the relatively simple shoulder gable. In this variation too the lower part is clearly neo-Renaissance in form.

First design

Executed design

Sketch of a Royal Palace 1891-92
Not realized

This 'sketch', later renamed 'fantasy' by Berlage himself and antedated 1888, depicts the front of a palace. At the end of 1891 the Maatschappij tot Bevordering der Bouwkunst announced a national competition to design a royal palace, this time in the vicinity of a major city. The inspiration for the idea was the association's fiftieth anniversary. The theme was similar to that proposed in 1885 [7] and attests to the intractability and longevity of the 'royal palace' problem in Amsterdam. It is likely Berlage considered competing, as he had earlier in 1885. For reasons unknown, however, he declined to enter. All that has been preserved of his ideas are two charcoal drawings and a fine wash drawing. The sketch is one of the finest examples of eclecticism in Dutch architecture. Forms from every period, including neo-styles, and numerous motifs from handbooks and portfolios of travel sketches are woven together into a picturesque, organic composition. In the stepped gable for the central section the tower of the office building for De Algemeene [14] is announced. This fantasy shows that by 1891 Berlage was by no means finished with eclecticism as a style for monumental buildings.

Schets

'tLootsje 1892
99 Rozengracht
Function: drinking hall, office and warehouse
Commissioned by: De Erven Lucas Bols

The present-day Lucas Bolshuis at 103 Rozengracht is the result of a renovation by Eduard Cuypers. Only the extreme left part with the shoulder gable was designed by Berlage: an alteration to the original factory building of De Erven Lucas Bols. Cuypers integrated Berlage's building into his designs and mirrored it in the right of the building. The stone tablet under the right-hand lesene of Berlage's façade bears the year of Cuypers' building (1902) too. The awning, which was originally only part of number 99, was continued by Cuypers, or perhaps later, so that it also covered the following entrance. The original hangers have disappeared, as has the seat that stood beside the entrance. Berlage's façade is thus still more or less in its original state. The entire interior has been moved to the village of Nieuw-Vennep, where the present-day offices of the Bols company are to be found.

When Berlage received the commission from De Erven Lucas Bols he was requested to design the façade and the interior of the drinking hall as much as possible in the spirit of the seventeenth century. The company was strongly traditional. It dated from 1575 and used this fact for publicity purposes. Furthermore, it had always been established in the same place in the city. In 1612 the original wooden building, 't Lootsje, was replaced by a stone building. This was on exactly the same spot where Berlage was now building. Berlage acceded to Bols' request and as a model he used the traditional seventeenth-century house with a shop on the ground floor. The 'shop'

Façade
[before 1902]

front is almost literally copied from such a house. The awning is suspended towards the façade, just above the door. Above this are leaded glass windows so that the high interior is well lit. This layout is purely traditional, but the details of the façade, such as the wrought-iron rods from which the awning is suspended and the 'tympanum' on the awning that marks the entrance, have Berlage's personal imprint. In continuing the awning across the other façade, this motif has been repeated in an arched form.

Berlage designed a neo-Renaissance-style brick façade above the shop front. A significant element in the Dutch Renaissance style, and one also used here, is the pilaster at the top of the façade and resting on a console. The rest of the façade's design is similarly conventional. On the first floor there are three cross-windows, two of which are topped with a segmental arch. In the middle of the second floor there is a loading hatch, set deeper than the two windows; the two windows are topped with basket arches. The façade of the attic floor consists only of a loading hatch with a rose window above it.

Gatehouse

The gatehouse designed later to the left of the façade has been demolished. It was built in a medieval-looking style; the actual entrance consisted of a double wooden door with a triple window above it. On top there were horizontal crenellations and a small saddle roof exactly as broad as the door opening. For the interior of the building Berlage designed panelling and furniture in the Dutch Renaissance style and combined these with tile tableaux and leaded glass windows. The floor was covered with black and white tiles, creating a chessboard pattern.

After this project, Berlage received commissions for similar drinking halls in other European cities. Eduard Cuypers was entrusted with the extension of 't Lootsje in 1900-03, however, probably because by then Berlage had built his modernistic Beurs, a building that did not fit in with the traditional image of De Erven Lucas Bols.

House 1892
72 Van Baerlestraat
Commissioned by: E.D. Pijzel

Although this house has been extensively altered, the upper façade has remained almost unchanged and shows that at the time Berlage was inspired by examples from rationalist architecture. The design is striking in its simplicity; it is stripped of all ornament. It is through the treatment of material and colour alone that all the structural elements acquire a greater aesthetic value. This is true, for example, of the deep tympani, which are placed under the relieving arches above the windows and display a woven pattern of yellow and red bricks. The same decorative element can be found in the Director's House of P.J.H. Cuypers' Rijksmuseum, dating from 1876-83. In using Cuypers' rationalist design theory Berlage wanted to show that the masonry in the tympani had no load-bearding function. The relieving arches themselves are also interesting; they are eloquently emphasized through the alternation of the red and yellow bricks and the simply profiled stone hoodmoulds. The façade is also enlivened by yellow glazed bricks fitted into the façade in a regular pattern, but it also retains a certain austerity, possibly because of the client's desire for a maximum of living space at a minimum of cost. This also explains the fact that the usual gable has been reduced to a dormer window, so that the entire width of the attic floor can be used as living space. The built design was preceded by a sketch. As far as the layout of the façade is concerned, this sketch largely corresponds to the executed design but is characterized by an even greater simplicity.

*Façade,
executed
design*

Algemeene Maatschappij van Levensverzekering en Lijfrente (De Algemeene) 1892-94
74-76 Damrak, 1-5 Baafjessteeg
Extended along Damrak and Nieuwendijk in 1901-05
Function: office building with shops
With: L. Zijl, sculptor
Demolished

This office building for De Algemeene insurance company was completed in 1894 and was to be of considerable importance for Berlage's career. His contemporaries' reactions to the design were unusually favourable. With this building Berlage made a name as the Netherlands' most progressive architect. The unanimous praise was probably related to the fact that, despite its modernity, the building displayed so many conventional characteristics that its formal language could still be read and understood. The structure of the façade prior to the later extension repeats that of the building for Focke & Meltzer [4]. The layout in bays is traversed by a vertical tripartite division: the ground floor with the large shop windows; the two central floors, which are treated as a unit; and the top floor, with a series of joined arched windows designed in a different style. At the top of the façade there is a board with the name of the company on the left, and, on the right, an asymmetric gable surmounted by a pelican. On the ridge of the high saddle roof is the word 'Algemeene' in large letters: this sign could be seen from as far as Central Station.

What is striking is the original design of the corner; never before had such a design been employed in Amsterdam. Apparently Berlage thought this solution so successful that he repeated the motif in the building for De

Nederlanden [16]. In a tabernacle on a high pedestal there is a statue of Johan de Witt sculpted by Bart van Hove. A lesene runs from the dome of the niche and develops into the console of the bay tower, which projects from the side wall. Unfortunately this pleasant and completely unacademic device disappeared when the building was extended. The corner solution is an early example of designing in an urban context; the street wall is optically closed off at the entrance to Baafjessteeg. The bay tower and the high side wall reinforce this effect. The sculpture was by L. Zijl, who was working with Berlage for the first time. The splendid staircase was provided with murals by Anton Derkinderen in 1900.

Between 1901 and 1905 the building was altered and extended in two stages. De Algemeene had bought a large number of buildings to the right and left on Damrak, and on Nieuwendijk; these were demolished to make way for an extension to Berlage's building. As a result, the new building covered a site five times larger than the original. Baafjessteeg was completely reshaped as an arcade. On Damrak the extension was carried out in the style of the original building. The façade on the Nieuwendijk, on the other hand, shows how Berlage's style had developed in the meantime. In its time the Cour, an inner court roofed with a glass dome next to the old staircase, was famous and often regarded as Berlage's most beautiful spatial creation. In 1963 the entire complex was demolished after a spectacular fire. It was replaced by the C & A building, which had opened its first Amsterdam shop, fitted out by Berlage, in this building in 1902.

*De Algemeene,
with extension
on Damrak
[1901-05]*

Beurspassage

Interior of Arti et Amicitiae 1893-94
112 Rokin
Function: club
With: A.C. Bleys
Commissioned by: Maatschappij Arti et Amicitiae

In 1840 the artists' association Arti et Amicitiae bought three buildings at the corner of Rokin and Spui in order to acquire its own exhibition space. It quickly became apparent that the space was unsuitable for this purpose, however, and in 1855 the complex was demolished. The present building was designed by the architect J.H. Leliman in 1856. In 1893 the board of the association decided to renovate the interior of the building. The aim was to have a more practical layout and also a completely new interior architecture and new furnishings. On 29 March 1893 the renovation was entrusted to A.C. Bleys and Berlage.

Bleys and Berlage made few changes to the exterior of the building, though the main entrance on Rokin was moved to Spui, which had recently been filled in, in order to improve the layout of the interior. The Old Dutch Renaissance style gateway that had been located there was converted into the main entrance. It was moved back again to the Rokin side during extensive restoration work in the early 1960s. As part of this restoration, the ground floor at the corner of Rokin and Spui was converted into shop space. The changes made by Berlage to the interior were more significant and have been preserved. As a result of moving the entrance, it became possible to separate the association's various functions better. Behind the new entrance on Spui there is a broad corridor, with, on the right, access to the offices of the board and the admin-

Clubroom

*Furniture
designed
for Arti et
Amicitiae*

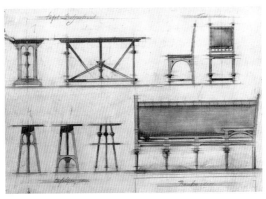

istration, and, on the left, doors to the other rooms, such as the library and the large clubroom, to which the cloakroom and the billiards room are joined. The latter can also be reached separately through a door at the end of the hall. The fixed architectural elements of the interior and also the furniture were designed in the Old-Dutch style, as a result of which Berlage achieved the unity in the interior he sought. The walls in the hall are covered with panelling, partly marble, partly wood. This is continued in the stairwell. The ceiling of the hall has wooden arches in groined and barrel forms; these recur in the wooden coving of the stairwell. The stairwell, illuminated by stained-glass windows, gives access to the exhibition rooms on the first floor. The interior of these rooms was hardly altered by Berlage. A skylight was added, however, to provide better lighting.

The clubrooms consist of a linked series of rooms that flow into each other. The transition from one room to the next is indicated visually by classical marble columns; these support the partition beams of the ceiling. Like the hall and the staircase, these rooms have wooden panelling. The panelled ceilings are decoratively painted. The motifs in the wallpaper are repeated in the curtains and hangings. The furniture in these rooms was also designed by Berlage. It is made from oak and is striking for its great variety of form. The style of the furniture can be described as neo-Renaissance with Gothic characteristics, the construction referring to the furniture of the Renaissance and the decorative motifs cut into the wood being derived from the Gothic. The wrought-iron lamps were also designed by Berlage. Finally, the finely worked fireplaces should also be mentioned; in execution and style they fit in with the design of the interior.

De Nederlanden van 1845 1894-95, extended in 1911
Muntplein (formerly Sophiaplein)
Function: shops, offices, photographic studio, caretaker's dwelling
With: L. Zijl, sculptor
Commissioned by: De Nederlanden van 1845

The office building for De Nederlanden, as it is now to be seen, dates from 1911. The area of the original building was then doubled by the extension on Kalverstraat and Rokin; this extension was also designed by Berlage. The attic floor on the corner of Kalverstraat and Muntplein was enlarged and the walls raised to provide a complete upper floor. The projecting top floor on Rokin originally housed a photographic studio. With the modifications of 1911 this floor was brought into the same plane as the façade; the layout of the windows, which had deviated here from that for the rest of the building, was also adapted. The original picturesque silhouette was replaced by an austere parapet, which was only interrupted by the tower containing the staircase and by crenellations at the corners. Only the buttress built against the façade at the bottom right, the loggia on the top left and the whimsical design of the top floors of the staircase tower in the middle recall the original design. In contrast to the 1911 extension, the building completed in 1895 [cover] was an original work of architecture. It was a manifesto against building in historical styles, in particular against the then dominant neo-Renaissance. In 1889-90 Evert Breman had built the first Amsterdam branch of De Nederlanden in this style on the same site. In structure and detail this building had shown many similarities to the shop building designed by the same architect on the corner of Reguliersbreestraat and Muntplein, opposite De

Nederlanden, so a comparison can still therefore be made.

Compared to Breman's competent stylistic exercise, Berlage's design was simply revolutionary. The special character of the building for De Nederlanden often causes us to forget that Berlage did not have a free hand in defining the floor-plan. The left-hand part of the new building had to be built on the foundations of Breman's building, so that the opening for the shop windows, the corner entrance, and the position of the staircase were already fixed. This is why the building looks like a complex of two corner buildings separated by a staircase tower. The effect of the architecture is to a great extent determined by the material, mainly brick and at structurally important places ashlar. As the plans for the façade show, Berlage was aiming at a compact architecture without relief. Even the projecting photographic studio and the buttress turn out, following the model of De Algemeene, to share a plane with the front of the building. The only enlivenment within the tight contour is provided by the wall openings, such as entrances, balconies and the loggia. Despite what the floor-plan would lead one to expect, the front is not symmetrically composed; its wings are brought into balance by the tower in the middle. The projecting photographic studio, for which one is prepared by the similarly projecting buttress below, and the complicated corner solution crowned by the loggia and the tower balance each other.

The characteristically, sharply defined silhouette was the goal: the skyline of the building was therefore rather complicated. The composition begins on Kalverstraat with a tiled roof; the gable corner is higher, and another tiled roof is wedged in between the gable corner and the

De Nederlanden [before extension]

staircase-tower. To the right of the tower the wall is again one-storey higher and the stepped skyline runs to the righthand corner of the building in order to end on the Rokin side in a straight line. This line contrasts elegantly with the simple outline that characterizes the lower part of the building.

The decoration is relatively restrained. The names of the businesses housed in the building are illustrated in coloured glazed bricks in the horizontal bands between the windows. On the right, beside the corner entrance, the personification of Insurance, which has killed the dragon, stands on a console; this symbolizes the promise to compensate for damage caused by fire. The winged console figure under the loggia is apparently a warning against fire. The buttress on the Rokin side is crowned by a griffin, which holds before it the coat of arms of De Nederlanden. A sow and piglets are carved in relief on the left of the interior walls of the main entrance, and similarly, to the right, chickens and chicks have been carved, probably as symbols of thriving prosperity. There are illustrations above the two entrances on the Rokin side; these are related to the type of business transacted by the shops: on the left there was originally a bodega and on the right (after the extension) a textile shop. Apart from having a thick cream-coloured layer of paint, the stairwell is for the most part still in its original state. Although not irretrievable, the atmosphere evoked in the beginning by the natural colours of the materials has disappeared.

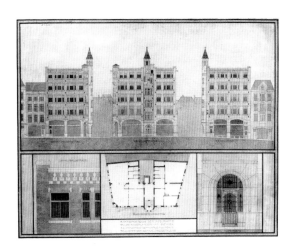

Design for De Nederlanden [1911]

Building plan for Museumplein 1895-96
Not realized

In 1895 Theodor Sanders, Berlage's former partner and, since 1887, director of the Noord-Hollandsche Tramweg Maatschappij, published a plan for a rail connection linking the south of Amsterdam to Haarlem. This project arose out of his plans, mainly unsuccessful up to then, for a network of trams for Amsterdam and its surroundings. Only the line to Purmerend, for which Berlage had designed the shelter [8], was ready by 1889. Like so many of Sanders' plans, the proposed new line to Haarlem showed great vision. As the terminus of the line, Sanders chose a piece of waste ground on Museumplein. Berlage made a rough design for the station building. It seems to be composed of buildings for De Nederlanden, which were designed at the same time [project 16 is one of these].

A station is of great significance to the development of an urban district. Berlage apparently foresaw this because he designed a building plan for the entire site behind the Rijksmuseum, with a park, a royal villa and a complex of 139 luxury dwellings – an enormous complex by Amsterdam's standards. Two blocks were planned on Paulus Potterstraat facing the Stedelijk Museum and a former villa site where the Van Gogh Museum and a number of private houses now stand.

The floor-plans and the layout of the site are unparalleled, in Amsterdam at least. Like that of the planned station, the architectural design is reminiscent of the building of De Nederlanden. In designing the layout of the street, Berlage tried to find an answer to the question of the 'boring streets and nice streets' ('langweilige und

kurzweilige Straßen') that was then attracting much attention, particularly in German periodicals. The two blocks are linked by a high gateway building. Perhaps the passage under the central section of the Rijksmuseum was the inspiration here. The gate is positioned quite far in front of the other façades and marks the end of the present-day Van de Veldestraat. The front of the block opposite the planned park is set back and forward rhythmically and ends in a higher corner section. The front of the block opposite the Stedelijk Museum has been set back creating a cour d'honneur, bordered with a shopping arcade. More justice would have been done to the façade of the Stedelijk Museum in this space than in the current situation. The long façade facing Jan Luykenstraat has been treated as a rear wall. Its length is only interrupted by a pronounced gateway entrance.

Dwellings and shops 1897
30-32 Raadhuisstraat
With: H. Bonda
Commissioned by: R. Cruyff

In 1897 the city council decided to sell a site on the north side of Raadhuisstraat, at the corner of Herengracht, to the contractor R. Cruyff. Two conditions were laid down: the building to be designed had to link up architecturally with the austere stone façade of the Gesticht van Liefdadigheid on Herengracht and it had to become a model for future building on Raadhuisstraat. The contractor developed the plan with the architect H. Bonda. Berlage designed the façades.

The building – whose façades, with the exception of the top of the tower, the changed layout of the shop windows and the replaced doors, are still in their original state – consists of four houses with shops built as one block. A high square tower on Herengracht links it to the blind wall of the Gesticht building. The steep gable with its angular shoulders drops towards the corner. This already exciting silhouette is continued on Raadhuisstraat with the almost uninterrupted plane of the tiled roof on a powerfully protruding console ledge, followed by an asymmetrical gable linked to the left by a parapet above the wall, which is higher here. The façade ends in an octagonal tower crowned with a cupola. The walls are rhythmically articulated by two bays, whose movement comes to rest in the equally projecting tower on Raadhuisstraat. The corner itself is interrupted with loggias, an idea also used in the building for De Nederlanden [16]; these provide a solid link between the two façades.

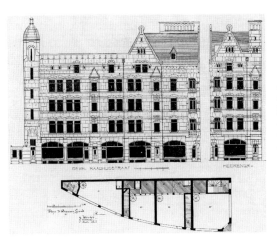

Façades and ground-floor plan Raadhuis-straat and Herengracht

Beurs and the layout of Beursplein 1896-1903
Damrak, Beursplein, Beursstraat, Oude Brugsteeg
With: L. Zijl and others
Commissioned by: city of Amsterdam

Berlage's Beurs, like all buildings designed as a manifesto, is a medium with its own message. The architecture of the Beurs says nothing about the stock exchange function for which it was constructed. Its message is the new architecture as image of a society renewing itself, a society forming the basis of a new culture. The Beurs' function as a medium for this message has turned out to be more durable than the original purpose of the building, the exchange of grain, stock and commodities.

The question of a new exchange building, which had been discussed since 1873, suddenly acquired a new urgency in 1895. In that year Treub become Alderman for Public Works, shortly after Weissman, the city architect, had been commissioned to rebuild Zocher's Beurs. Weissman's plans were unsatisfactory, however, and Berlage was therefore invited to take on the commission in February 1896. Instead of modifying Zocher's Beurs, Berlage, at the instigation of Treub, immediately drew up plans for a new building. To avoid delays and an irksome debate about the architectural qualities of his design, the plans were kept secret – the Beurs committee itself was empowered to assess only the floor-plans. It was not until March 1898 that the city council agreed to the plans being published. Their publication came as a bolt from the blue. The design was already complete and Berlage's critics and opponents were too late to be able to influence the course of events. In May the work had already been contracted out, and building began in the same month.

*Perspective
of the Beurs*
[1897]

*Perspective
of the Beurs*
[1902]

DE·NIEUWE·BEURS·OP·HET·DAMRAK·TE·AMSTERDAM·GEZIEN·KOMENDE·VAN·DEN·DAM·

Five years later, on 27 May 1903, the new Beurs was opened.

Berlage repeatedly altered the plans, even during the period of construction. An important role in this was played by the poet Verwey, who, with an eye to the programme of symbolic arts to be executed by Zijl, Derkinderen, J. Toorop, R.N. Roland Holst and J. Mendes da Costa, researched the history of Amsterdam trade and provided the Beurs with poetic texts. This intensive dialogue between poet and architect was inspired by the collaboration of Alberdingk Thijm and P.J.H. Cuypers in the building of the Rijksmuseum. On the basis of this, but largely because after the initial designs Berlage arrived at a completely new interpretation of the commission, the original design was to undergo fundamental changes. The architectural form became simpler. In the completed building Berlage succeeded in welding the many design ideas originating in the work of Cuypers and derived from old Italian, Dutch and more recent American examples into a coherent whole. In the first series of designs, Berlage was using as his point of departure the 'church building'. For instance, the tower and the entrance arches on Beursplein, the only remnants of what was originally designed as an apse, were inspired by such Romanesque churches as Sint Servaas in Maastricht. The building actually built, on the other hand, was inspired by the medieval town hall of northern Italy (the Palazzo Vecchio in Florence, the Palazzo Pubblico in Siena), and van Campen's Town Hall.

The change in Berlage's conception of the design is related to two events. At the end of 1897 Berlage was commissioned to draw up plans for a new building for the ANDB, the diamond workers' union. Berlage was thus

*Relief above
Beursplein
entrance*

*Tile tableau
'Present' in
the entrance
hall of the
Beurs, Jan
Toorop*

designing for labour as well as capital. Already in the case of the ANDB building the architect was drawing on Italian models, and he ultimately designed a people's palace that was unmistakably influenced by the Bargello in Florence, the earliest monument of a democratic constitution. Secondly, in the course of 1897-98 Berlage and Verwey began to change their views on the function of an exchange building. They were convinced that social change would make stock exchange activity unnecessary, and that it would have to make way for other forms of exchange and distribution of goods and capital. Berlage therefore consciously designed a building that would outlive its original function; in contrast to the people's palace of the ANDB, he designed a palace that was also to represent the city of Amsterdam, the heart of the Netherlands: it was to be a symbolic town hall.

There is virtually nothing to identify the Beurs as a stock exchange. Only in the gable on Beursplein is it stated, in small letters, that this Beurs was completed in 1902. Other decorations make the Beurs an unmistakable comment on the class-ridden society of the time. A quatrain by Verwey, for example, calls on the brokers to consider the meaning of their activities by pointing out that there are many other ways of providing the necessities of life. In the vestibule (an entrance-hall lobby signifying a court or tribunal) one can still see three tile tableaux by Toorop illustrating the theme of past, present, and future. The divided class society of 1900 is depicted in the background of the middle tableau. The commodities exchange is also intended as a reception or banqueting hall and this connotation is reinforced by references to the Palazzo della Ragione, 'Il Salone', in Padua and Palladio's Basilica in Vicenza. These references in-

DE·GOEDERENBEURS·IN·DE·NIEUWE·BEURS·TE·AMSTERDAM

Commodities exchange

Ground-floor plan

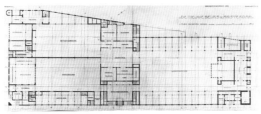

clude, among other things, the surrounding galleries.

Despite its formidable complexity, the Beurs was an architectural unity. Nevertheless, the four outer walls are articulated in completely different ways. They correspond to the varying character of the surrounding street spaces and show, as it were, four different aspects of the design. The monumental façade oriented to Beursplein, also designed by Berlage, is self-sufficient. The colossal corner tower already announces the completely different relations and the larger spatial scale of the Stationsplein-Dam axis. The façade refers to the old town hall of Amsterdam, which was replaced in the seventeenth century by that of van Campen. The form of this building is widely known because of an often-copied painting by Saenredam and numerous engravings. The expression of the building on Damrak is completely different. The silhouette refers to P.J.H. Cuypers' Central Station, but the façade is completely flat, rhythmically articulated only by the position of the windows; the dimensions of the bays are derived from the original scale of the buildings on the other side of the street.

In contrast to the 150-metre-long Damrak façade, the northern façade facing the water is open. Seen from the railway station, the Beurs looks like a city, complete with gates, city wall, gables and towers. The model for this unusual harbour front was the western façade of the Rijksmuseum, which Berlage repeated here in reverse and changed so much in the course of the design process that its origin is hardly recognizable any more. On the fourth side of the building Beursstraat runs slightly oblique in relation to Damrak, the façade on Oude Brugsteeg being broader than the southern façade; the floor-plan of the Beurs is thus a trapezium, with rooms that are generally rectangular and grouped parallel to Damrak.

Apart from some minor renovations and the fact that the Beursstraat façade is now blighted by a factory chimney and a pedestrian bridge to the new Effectenbeurs, the Beurs' exterior is still in its original state. The numerous colourfully painted wall brackets date from 1909, however, when the structure of the building had to be strengthened because dangerous cracks had appeared as a consequence of irregular subsidence caused by the ground settling. Far-reaching alterations to the interior were necessary, and this led in particular to the extremely daring reconstruction of the commodities exchange. To preserve this space drastic measures were necessary, but since Berlage himself designed the modifications (which included the division of the arches in the side walls by constructing an extra column in the middle of each span, and the fitting of tie rods between the trusses of the roof) the atmosphere of this hall has been retained.

As a consequence of the recent transformation of the northern part of the Beurs into a music centre with two concert halls, the vestibule on Beursplein into a café, and the commodities exchange into an exhibition hall, many alterations to the interior have had to be carried out. P. Zaanen was the architect responsible for these.

Algemeene Nederlandsche Diamantbewerkers Bond (ANDB)
1898-1900
3-9 Henri Polaklaan (formerly Plantage Franschelaan)
Function: union building
Commissioned by: board of the ANDB

The ANDB, founded in 1894, developed within a few years to become the most powerful trade union in the Netherlands. In 1897 the board decided to commission the construction of new offices. Berlage's definitive design was completed in 1899. The most impressive motif is the tower, protruding high above its bourgeois surroundings. The monumental flight of steps, the stone bollards, the crenellations and the high tower immediately announced that this was more than a house or an office building. The building's special character is further reinforced by the completely flat façade and the large size of brick used, the so-called *reuzenmoppen*, used particularly in medieval times. The architecture of the building is carefully integrated into the street wall; the front is precisely in the building line, and to determine the height of the façade Berlage continued the line of the cornice of the house on the left-hand side and crowned it with crenellations. The façade of the four-storey building is articulated by rectangular triple windows, which decrease in height towards the upper floors. Heavy stone lintels together with the barely articulated plinth, the crenellations and the initials of the trade union placed there at regular intervals just below provide a horizontal countermovement.

The spatial layout of the interior has been clarified in a simple manner. The printing works were formerly located in the basement, with a separate entrance on the

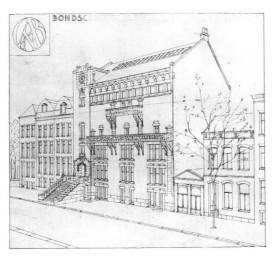

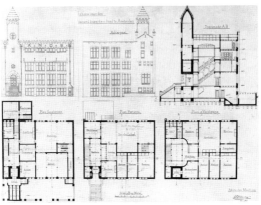

*First design
[1898]*

*Floor-plans
and façade of
the executed
design
[1899]*

right. The staircase on the raised ground floor lies on the axis of the steps; to the right are offices and rooms for public functions. The remarkable height of this floor draws attention to the former meeting room of the union board, the governing body of the ANDB, at the rear. The steps therefore have the same function as the steps or the balcony of a town hall; it was from here that members of the board could address the workers and speeches could be given. The two upper floors were intended for offices and the library.

In typological terms the union building is related to such thirteenth-century Italian town halls as the Palazzo del Podesta in Florence or the Palazzo dei Priori in Volterra, which Berlage interpreted as monuments of popular sovereignty. The simple rectangular contour without sculptural additions, the crenellations, and in particular the architectural treatment of the tower all suggest this. The tower was not designed, as was usual in Dutch architecture, as an independent component of the building; instead it is included in the plane of the façade. Only at the level of the crenellations does the tower separate itself from the façade and acquire its own character. It symbolizes the watchfulness and the power of the organized working class, a symbol echoed by the monumental steps that elevate the worker, literally and figuratively, the impressive entrance arch with the emblem of the ANDB above it, and the diamond-shaped lantern in the round window high up in the tower.

The union building appears as a people's palace, and its rugged character reminded many of a fortress. The façade of the offices betrays many different sources of inspiration, though the building is firmly rooted in the Dutch tradition, despite the evidence of Italian influence.

*Façade
Henri
Polaklaan*

The open basement is Dutch, although Berlage rejected the custom of designing this more or less monumentally as a plinth on which the building rises. Further Berlage includes a reference to the seventeenth- and eighteenth-century patrician houses of the Golden Bend in Amsterdam, which consist of a basement, a high *piano nobile* and two upper floors, diminishing in height, and decorated with a plinth, pilasters, mouldings and cornices; they sometimes had an attic too. Berlage ostentatiously omitted classicistic decoration in favour of a purely structural, completely flat façade, however, because he regarded the representational and decorative forms of Dutch Classicism as signs of creative weakness and architectural degeneration. He translated the working class's struggle against the bourgeoisie into an architectural critique of the monuments that most purely represent its quest for power. This critique manifests itself in an attempt to surpass the language of bourgeois architecture without using the symbols considered necessary by the bourgeoisie to indicate status.

The stairwell of the building is behind the closed front of the tower, accessible through a quite dark, vaulted enclosed porch in which a revolving door was later placed. It is as if the interior is secured against the outside world by formidable, thick walls. If the idea of the fortress or castle is confirmed by the first few steps inside, after traversing the entrance the visitor undergoes a completely unexpected spatial sensation: one then enters the *cour*, a bright inner court, three stories high. Light streams through the glass roof, gradually lessening in intensity, while the rooms behind the arches of the arcades that surround the court are in shadow. The walls of the staircase and gallery are decorated with yellow and white glazed bricks so that a regular textile-like pattern is created. The walls in the court are mainly yellow with white-blue strips under the balustrades; the arches of the arcade are accentuated by yellow and white bricks. This colour scheme fills the inner court with a sunny warmth.

The building has undergone many changes and additions in the course of the years. Only the staircase and the boardroom on the first floor are in their original state. Extensive alterations were carried out in 1959 and 1979; even the bollards at the front were removed to make space for parking. Only recently was the monumental value of Berlage's creation rediscovered. In 1986 the building was designated a trade union museum. The necessary alterations and extremely modest restorations were carried out in 1990 according to a design by Atelier Pro.

Extension to Bible Hotel 1899
Beursplein (formerly Damrak)
Commissioned by: W.P. Werker
Not realized

The Bible Hotel was originally at Warmoesstraat. After Damrak was filled in, A.J. van Arkel built an extension with a monumental façade on Damrak in 1891. The extension Berlage (or most probably an unidentified member of his bureau) designed in 1899 was to have been to the right of this façade, and, in contrast to van Arkel's design, the floor-plans of the extension did not extend to Warmoesstraat. We have sketchy floor-plans of only the *piano nobile* and the attic floor, and a vertical elevation. The *piano nobile* itself consists mainly of a smoking and card room. The attic floor is recognizable by the small corner balcony and contains rooms for the staff. A vertical shaft through the centre of the building ensures sufficient light. In the basement there is a kitchen, storage room and a beer cellar, accessible through a door in the side wall.

The style and layout of the original façade and the extension do not correspond. Van Arkel built in a neo-Renaissance style; the extension is much simpler. Furthermore, the design of the latter had one floor more than the existing building; it is not clear from the drawings whether this extension was to be higher than the original building. We do not know why the extension was never built.

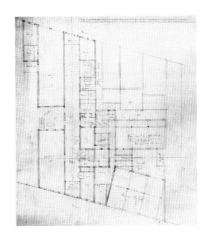

Plan of
piano nobile

Façade

Koning & Bienfait 1900, extended in 1908
104 Da Costakade
Function: building materials research laboratory
Commissioned by: Koning & Bienfait

The façade of this building, which still houses the original firm, has not been altered since 1908. In that year Berlage added two new floors, as a result of which the height of the building was almost the same as that of adjacent buildings. The new attic floor was for storage, the third floor was intended for the metallography department. Here, in contrast to the small windows of the original 1900 façade, a single window covers almost the entire width of the façade. The unusual form, broad, under a gentle arch, is probably a reference to the ground-floor and first-floor windows in the façade of number 102. Nevertheless, in order to ensure a degree of unity between the large horizontal window and the small vertical windows, Berlage placed the mullions of the large window in line with those between the small windows on the lower floors. The windows of the original façade are placed in groups of two and three. This reflects the disposition of the spaces behind. Hence, too, the entrance, a portico with a semicircular arch, is not in the middle but to the left. The façade is built from brick. There is hardly any decoration, the use of stone is frugal. The tiles along the façade above the ground floor showing the company's name add some colour: yellow and orange for the base and blue for the letters. A similar tableau with the text 'Proefstation voor Bouwmaterialen' disappeared in the alterations, as did the open parapet at the top of the original façade.

Façade
[1900]

Façade
[1908]

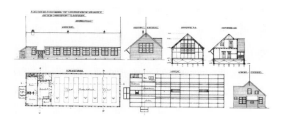

Design school with caretaker's dwelling 1900
Derde Conradstraat
Commissioned by: Vereniging De Eenheid
Demolished

The school has a simple floor-plan and is covered with a saddle roof. To the right of the entrance there is a single elongated drawing hall, to the left a caretaker's dwelling. The building borders a timberyard at the back, which is why there is only a series of windows at the front extending the whole length of the building. To increase the amount of light even further, there is a large composite window in the short side. The enclosed vestibule provides access to both the drawing hall and the caretaker's dwelling. The latter consists of a ground floor and an attic floor. There is a kitchen, a room and a toilet on the ground floor, and there are some bedrooms in the attic. The attic floor covers only a small part of the area of the whole building. In order to create space for the stairway and a bedroom the building incorporates an extension at the rear.

Villa Parkwyck 1900; De Bilt *c.* 1913
90 Van Eeghenstraat (demolished and rebuilt at Soestdijkschen
Straatweg, De Bilt, now 319 Soestdijkseweg, Bilthoven)
Function: residence
Commissioned by: L. Simons

This villa has an unusual history. It was originally built in
1900 for L. Simons, director of the Maatschappij voor
Goede en Goedkope Lectuur (an association for 'quality
and inexpensive reading') (later the Wereldbibliotheek).
The house was soon nicknamed 'the teapot' or 'the house
with the handle' because of a curved flue that ran from
the kitchen to the chimney. The neighbours were not im-
pressed with the house, but the professional community
was. When Simons sold it in 1913 the new owner wanted
to make so many changes – the kitchen extension had to
go, a floor had to be added, all the windows had to be of
plate glass – that Berlage refused to co-operate. Ultimately the building was bought by the architect J.B.
Lambeek jun. with the intention of demolishing it and
rebuilding it in De Bilt. This time Berlage agreed to co-
operate. The result can thus be seen as a legitimate creation, despite criticism of the changes carried out. The
villa, which was rebuilt on the Soestdijkschen Straatweg
in 1913-14, is still in good condition and is a listed building. The harmony between the floor-plan and the façade
of the original building on the Van Eeghenstraat arose
from the design method, which Berlage was probably
using here for the first time for both the floor-plan and the
elevation. He used a square module, which was not confined to a plane but must be seen as an imaginary cube.
This cube determined not only the layout of the floor-
plan and the façades, but also the volumes of the various

rooms. The use of a grid can easily be seen in the floor-plan and the window layout of the walls. These walls are austere and flat, a fact emphasized by the deep-set windows. They end in three projecting layers of brick right under the roof edges. The roof itself was basically a hipped roof, with a half hipped roof for the kitchen. The white columns at the entrance and the gutters are decoratively painted. The lintel above the entrance portico bares the name of the villa.

The layout, characterized by Berlage himself as 'odd', was determined by the location of the villa next to the Vondelpark; at the original location the living rooms are oriented to the park because of the view, and as a result of this the kitchen faces on to the street. The ground floor consists of kitchen, parlour, drawing-room, dining-room, and study. The walls of the drawing-room are papered, the other rooms on this floor have painted walls. All the ceilings are of wood. The hall is panelled in glazed stone, above which there are ornamental stones. The bedrooms and bathroom are located on the first floor, the servants' rooms are in the attic. In its Amsterdam location the garden was laid out in keeping with the character of the house.

Villa Parkwyck, Amsterdam

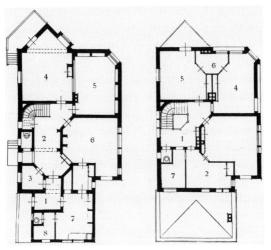

Villa Parkwyck, Amsterdam: ground-floor- and first-floor plan

Amsterdamsch Wisselkantoor 1901

95 Damrak, corner of Damraksteeg (number 96, with which it formed a pair, was demolished in 1985)

Function: exchange office, office space, lunchroom and bodega

Commissioned by: De Amsterdamsche Bank

Of the building Berlage built in 1901 for the Amsterdamsch Wisselkantoor, only the right-hand part with the gable, number 95 Damrak, has been preserved. The four buildings, 95 to 98, have been combined in such a way that they provide a short 'architectural history after Berlage'. Berlage's mellow yellow building on the right-hand side was the starting point. At the extreme left is a building by A.J. Kropholler and J.F. Staal from 1909 – they built more in the style of Berlage than Berlage himself. Between these is a contemporary interpretation. The left-hand side of Berlage's original building was demolished in 1985 to make way for this middle section. The new building refers to Berlage's, but this does not prevent the loss of the balance the 1901 building possessed.

The original building has a regular façade beneath a saddle roof on the left-hand side, and becomes more varied towards the right. It ends in a square bay structure, which juts forward on the first floor, supported by a heavy console. From that point on, the volume of the corner increases, to decrease after the third floor and end in a pyramidic roof. This theme climaxes above in the gable of the right-hand part of the building. The line of the bay roof continues in the line of the gable, so that the whimsical volume does not disturb the composition as a whole. Berlage had earlier used this design motif in the buildings for De Algemeene and De Nederlanden. The quiet half of the building paves the way so to speak for the bulging

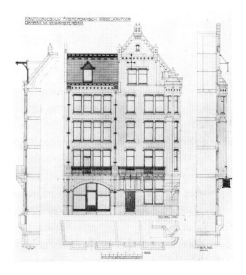

Façade

Situation
[1984]

development of the bay. This effect was made even stronger after the building was altered, as a result of which the balcony, which ran over the entire width of the building on the first floor, was demolished and replaced by a double bay.

The division can probably be explained by the fact that the commission was originally confined to the foreign exchange department in the right-hand part of the building. An earlier façade design covered only this part of the final building and is less complicated. The division is also to be seen in the floor-plan of the ground floor. The lunchroom/bodega De Beursbengel was located on the left, the actual exchange office was on the right; the upper floors were used as offices. The façade is built of light, yellow brick, and Berlage characteristically used stone too, in this case red sandstone. The supports on which the stone rests at the window openings were given extra emphasis by white and orange glazed bricks. After various alterations over the years, nothing has remained of the original interior of the building. Only the exchange office was fitted out with any luxury; the counter and other furniture was of teak. The stairwell was finished with glazed brick.

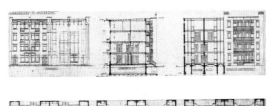

Façades, ground-, first-, and second-floor plans

Four houses 1902

Frans van Mierisstraat

Commissioned by: Coöperatieve Bouwvereniging Eigen Haard

Not realized

The four houses are treated as two square blocks built together. Each block is twelve metres wide; the floor-plan and elevation of the two blocks are identical. The commission envisaged middle-class dwellings of around 100 square metres. Each dwelling has its own staircase, two per portico. The dwellings on the ground floor and first floor cover the whole block; the two dwellings above are only six metres wide, but run over two floors. This difference is clearly articulated in the placing of the balconies. The floor-plans have been sketchily developed; the façade is a bit dull. Apparently this commission failed to inspire Berlage, or a draughtsman at his bureau, to pioneering achievement.

Building on the site of the old stock exchange *c.* 1903
Damrak, on the site of the present-day Bijenkorf
Not realized

The old Beurs by J.D. Zocher on the corner of the Dam and Damrak was demolished in 1903. During the period of demolition Berlage drew up a number of designs for this site, for a booksellers' exchange, a hotel and a department store respectively. He was interested in designing buildings for this site because of its strategic position next to his new Beurs [19], the Amsterdam Wisselkantoor [25], and the building for De Algemeene [14], immediately opposite the Beurs on Damrak. The character and volume of this new building were supposed to echo those of Berlage's other buildings.

The designs consist mainly of floor-plans, one of which is signed by Berlage. It is possible that some of the designs were made by staff at his bureau. In the designs for a booksellers' exchange, the exchange activity is mainly confined to the ground floor, while the stock room is always at the back of the building. Shops to be rented separately were planned on the ground floor facing Damrak. All the designs have a ground-floor café with a conference hall above it facing the Dam. The function of the other floors differs in each design. For example, there is a plan for a hotel and one for offices. The various functions envisaged on the upper floors have separate entrances and staircases, probably with the aim of maximizing the extent to which the site could be utilized.

There is only one drawing with elevations. This shows the façades on Damrak and the Dam. The elevations do not correspond with the surviving floor-plans. The left-hand part of the façade on Damrak shows similarities to

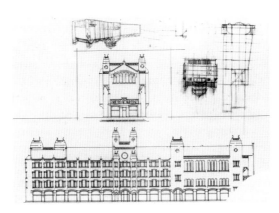

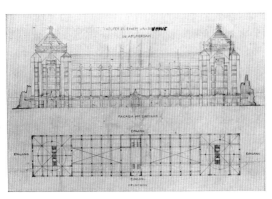

Sketch for a booksellers' exchange

'Project zu einem Waarenhaus'

the façade of the Nieuwendijk extension to the De Alge-meene building. This similarity is mainly in the form and layout of the windows. On this basis the drawing can be dated to around 1903. There are also perspective sketches drawn in pencil on this sheet; these resemble the vertical elevation of another building, the 'Project zu einem Waarenhaus'. This design probably dates from 1904. On 19 March of that year the journal *Architectura* announced that the city of Amsterdam was negotiating with a German *Waarenhaus* for the sale of the old Beurs site. The company concerned, Tietz, a large German de-partment store, wanted to open a branch in Amsterdam. Berlage's bureau probably made the design on its own initiative. Apart from the elevation mentioned earlier, the drawing shows a floor-plan of the ground floor; the de-tails were probably the responsibility of one of Berlage's staff. The actual shop front is related to designs by the German and Austrian architects B. Sehring and J.M. Olbrich. This can be seen especially in the vertical articu-lation of the large glass surfaces. The name of the com-pany is on both towers.

Nieuwe Amstelbrug 1899-1903, 1986
Continuation of Ceintuurbaan
Commissioned by: Department of Public Works, city of Amsterdam

In March 1986 the Nieuwe Amstelbrug was reopened after being completely rebuilt in its original state. It was first opened on 5 June 1903. The design is by the Department of Public Works, and it was adapted by Berlage in 1900. Berlage believed public utilities like bridges should be sparsely decorated. His architecture was therefore also simple: the decoration was confined to the street furniture. The later, green-painted castiron railings, originally supposed to close off the bridge to traffic, are still there, though they are no longer used. Their function has been assumed by red and white barriers. The railings are not by Berlage but P.L. Kramer, who designed many bridges for the Department of Public Works. The bridge has seven bays, with the middle one built as a double bascule bridge. There are semicircular extensions on either side of the moveable section of the bridge; from here the bridgeman can operate the mechanism to raise and lower the bridge. The fixed part of the bridge is formed on both sides by three brick arches, supported by stone piers; the arches are finished in stone. A simple brick parapet with rectangular openings and topped with ashlar runs along the entire length of the bridge; it continues to the banks in a long, splendid curve. The image of the bridge, and therefore of this part of the Amstel, is most strongly defined by the characteristic green-painted cast-iron electrified masts for the street lamps and trams. On one or both sides of these masts there is an arch from which a lamp hangs.

Alterations and extension to Ons Huis 1904

8 Rozenstraat (formerly 8-32 Rozenstraat)

Function: gymnastics hall, clubrooms, caretaker's flat and second stairwell

Commissioned by: Vereniging Ons Huis

In 1892 C.B. Posthumus Meyjes sen. built a club building for Ons Huis; this building was extended by Berlage in 1904. The extension was intended mainly to house a large gymnastics hall and a caretaker's flat, but the heart of the extension was a second stairwell, necessary because of the considerable danger of fire caused by the top-floor theatre in Posthumus Meyjes' building. Berlage's extension is small, between the original building and Zoutkeetsteeg, which was then a dead-end alley. Only the bay above the right-hand entrance is by Berlage. His extension to the rear of the building is somewhat broader though. The building still looks as it did after Berlage's alterations, though the interior has been modified considerably over the years. P. Blom recently made entresols, finished in plain wood and wire glass, for example.

Probably at the request of Ons Huis, Berlage adapted his designs for the façade completely to Posthumus Meyjes' neo-Renaissance style. He used the same window forms and relieving arches and retained the cornice; in the roof itself he set an identical dormer window. The window layout has been changed however. Ons Huis' request apparently did not cover the side wall, a place where one does not normally indulge in decoration. Here, and in the interior, therefore, he displayed the style that resembles his other work from that period.

Berlage divided the extension into three units: the front of the building, which houses among other things the stairwell, the middle section, and the back of the building – where the gymnastics hall was located. The hall has its own entrance on Zoutkeetsteeg. The front part of the building consists of five floors (including the ground floor and the attic floor), one more than in Posthumus Meyjes' building, while the height of the original building and the extension is the same. Posthumus Meyjes' storeys are very high, typical of the nineteenth century. Berlage did not need such height to ensure sufficient light, however, because the rooms are comparatively shallow on account of the staircase behind. The result of having an extra floor is that the floor level of the extension does not link up with that of the original building. Furthermore, the floors of the new front part are not on the same level as the middle and rear parts. Complicated split-level constructions are needed to resolve the differences in level and to create enough new spaces on such an extremely small piece of ground.

Despite all the alterations, there are still details that are recognizably Berlage's. The current user, the national COC (an association representing lesbians and gays), has attempted to preserve the original state of the building as much as possible. The stairwell is probably the best preserved; it has always been plastered, except for the arches of clean masonry. On entering, one immediately sees the initials of Ons Huis, an 'O' in which a 'H' is set. Such initials are often seen in Berlage's works, for example in the ANDB building [20]. Similar carvings along the stairs are to be found in Villa Hingst [34]. The panelling of one of the clubrooms is still intact. For the stairwell Berlage used the colours green and red, the rest of the building is brown with yellow blocks.

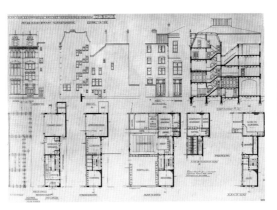

*Façades,
section and
floor-plans*

Shops and dwellings 1904
4-8 Hobbemastraat, corner of Schapenburgerpad
Commissioned by: De Algemeene

As was the case with Raadhuisstraat [18], this building provided shops and dwellings for the prosperous middle class. The spatial layout of the block can be read from the layout of the façade. The bays above the entrance doors indicate three upper dwellings and, according to Berlage's language, also indicate where the stairwells, unusually spacious in this case, are located deeper in the building. The façades of the shop fronts and upper floors contrast sharply. This can still be seen, despite the later alterations to the shop fronts. At the ground floor the massive wall of the dwellings is reduced to brick piers, which bear both the bays and the large segmental arches of the shop fronts. The shop windows are set deep into the wall, while the windows of the intermediate floor and those of the dwellings above project. The façade appears to tilt forward. This effect is strengthened by the top of the wall between the two fronts on the left (now faced with stone slabs): the pilaster has been set back, the capital and the impost, on the other hand, are in the same plane as the façade. The bays, an important feature in this design, have been arranged as independent volumes; they apparently cleave their way through the wall surface and intersect the brick frieze and cornice with their pyramidic roofs.

Façade
Hobbema-
straat

Floor-plan

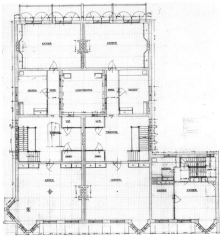

Shops and dwellings 1905
74-96 Linnaeusstraat, 1-2 Pretoriusstraat

The Transvaal neighbourhood is still comparatively isolated. Pretoriusstraat is an important access road from the east. In 1903 Berlage had already designed a traffic square at the point where this street meets Linnaeusstraat; the square is symmetrically laid out, and Pretoriusstraat functions as an axis. In doing so, Berlage was inviting the building sector to take out long leases on the sites on either side of the square and build two identical blocks, whose walls would form both a forecourt and a sort of entrance gateway to the new neighbourhood. Two years later a building developer gave Berlage the opportunity to realize his ideas.

The design is exceptional in Berlage's *œuvre* from the early years of this century. The design of the complex, completely symmetrical in its main outlines and details, anticipates his later work, which came to be increasingly influenced by town-planning considerations; his thinking in terms of axes, typical of the baroque, is particularly significant here. The two blocks offer space for four and three shops respectively, with dwellings above. Spacious middle-class dwellings are located on the square; two per floor, reached by staircase bays. The narrow buildings next to the corners on Linnaeusstraat and Pretoriusstraat include smaller dwellings. The floor-plans, particularly those of these smaller dwellings, did not comply with the regulations laid down shortly after by the city. Stairwells that were not directly connected to the open air and rooms that could easily be converted into alcoves were forbidden under these regulations.

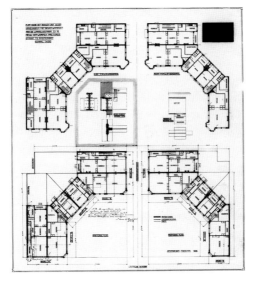

*North block,
Pretorius-
plein*

Floor-plans

Oosterspeeltuin 1905, 1911

Czaar Peterstraat

Function: neighbourhood facilities

Commissioned by: Vereniging De Oosterspeeltuin

Public library (1905) *demolished c.* 1960; gymnastics hall (1911), bathhouse (date unknown) *neither realized*

Vereniging De Oosterspeeltuin, founded in 1902, was one of the first organizations in Amsterdam to be dedicated to popular education, improving hygienic conditions, neighbourhood facilities and to setting up playgrounds. It belonged to the same ideological tradition as Ons Huis. Berlage was on the board of the association, as were Simons and Wibaut among others. This explains his involvement in this unimpressive commission.

In 1905 he designed the first building, a library; it has only a ground floor, which contains the reading room, a storeroom and toilets. There is an open veranda at the back. The building was built partly in brick and partly in wood. The helm roof was covered in tiles; it also has a small roof turret with a ventilation cap on the ridge. The veranda is accessible from the reading room via two double doors. Between these is a brick chimney, decorated with glazed tiles; a clock was set into the chimney. The building's function should not be compared with that of a contemporary library. Many people were illiterate at that time, and therefore meetings were often arranged at which someone read out loud. The gymnastics hall and the bathhouse were designed in a similar style; they were never built, however, probably due to a lack of money.

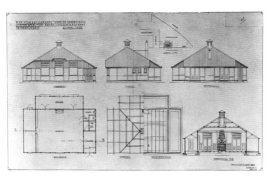

Public library

House 1906
148 Middenweg
Commissioned by: S. Walewijk

It is a long time since Villa Walewijk was a residence; it now houses offices. Along with the change in function, the façades and interior have undergone far-reaching alterations. Contrary to Berlage's principles, the brick walls are now covered with a layer of dark brown paint. The layout of the windows has been completely changed, some have even been bricked up. The windows could originally be closed off with red and white shutters. The top panes of the windows were of leaded glass. Despite all the changes, the original character of the villa is still recognizable in the half hipped roof, the entrance porch and the small wooden balcony on the left-hand side of the façade.

In 1906 Berlage made two designs, of which the more spacious variation was built. The house consists of two floors, a ground floor and a floor under the roof. In the first design the façade is partially panelled in wood just under the roof and has an extension with an arch-formed opening on either side of the front. In the drawings for this house it is possible to see the changes carried out in the ultimate design: the entrance was moved from the side wall to the front, the living room was enlarged, and the balcony room acquired a dormer window. The house was built in a semi-rural style, which was appropriate to the surroundings. At that time Watergraafsmeer consisted entirely of meadows. The form of the roof and the treatment of the entrance show some affinity with Villa Parkwyck [24].

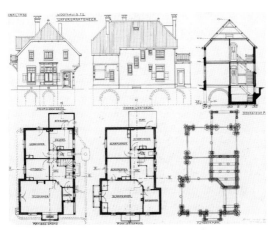

*Façades,
section and
floor-plans of
the executed
design*

House 1907
18 Koninginneweg
Commissioned by: A. Hingst

This villa is built on a small slope, and Berlage therefore had to provide a solution to a difference in levels. From the entrance porch the kitchen is accessible via a short set of stairs going down, while the living-room floor is reached by a short set of stairs going up. The living rooms are on the first floor; the ground floor, which is connected directly to the garden at the back, houses the kitchen and a room overlooking the garden. In order to avoid any further complications with split-levels, Berlage positioned the entrance porch forward of the rest of the floor-plan. The front is rather closed, almost repellant, since the living-room floor has been placed on a base containing a windowless cellar-like storage space. The rear of the house, clearly visible from Koningslaan, is striking for its great openness; it has many large windows. This difference can be explained in terms of the more 'public' front of the house on the street and the 'private' part facing the garden.

The villa is built in brick, with ashlar at the corners of the window frames and above the mullions. The hallway is of a sober luxury. The walls are clad with yellow and white glazed bricks. On the floor there are coloured tiles laid in a geometric pattern. There is parquet and wooden panelling throughout the house, except in the kitchen, bathroom and toilets, which have a floor similar to that of the entrance porch. Simple geometric motifs in leaded glass decorate the top panes of some windows. These details clearly show how Berlage's quest for unity was not confined to the façade or floor-plan.

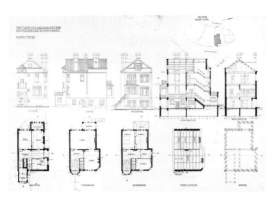

Façades,
sections and
floor-plans

Arbeiders Coöperatie De Dageraad 1907-08
1-7 Toldwarsstraat, Tolstraat, Pieter Aertszstraat (formerly Nieuwe Tolstraat)
Function: commercial premises with thirteen dwellings
With: J.W.F. Hartkamp

De Dageraad, founded in 1901, was a co-operative society that baked and distributed bread and sold groceries. The co-operative was supported by the labour movement in Amsterdam, in which the diamond workers' union (ANDB) played a leading role. In 1907 the board of De Dageraad had commissioned the architect J.W.F. Hartkamp to design a new co-operative building; Hartkamp had already made a reputation with his design for the typefoundry Tetterode (1903) at 163 Bilderdijkstraat and with a building of the same year at 37 Damrak. The *schoonheidscommissie*, an official body that advises, in particular, on the external appearance of new buildings, objected, and the most important financier, the ANDB, made certain demands concerning the architectural designs and recommended Berlage as architect. Ultimately the board of De Dageraad accepted under protest, and Berlage was asked to design the façades. He made only a few changes to Hartkamp's floor-plan.

The main façade of the U-shaped complex is on Toldwarsstraat. The division of the masses is for the most part symmetrical, with the staircase tower in the middle serving as an axis. On the other hand, other elements, especially the window grouping and the position of the stairwell bays, are asymmetric. The actual co-operative building is in between the two housing wings. It is characterized by the tower, a high façade, at the top of which were originally the words 'Arbeiders Coöperatie', a de-

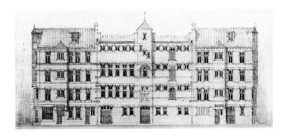

*Façade
Toldwars-
straat*

viating floor height and a functional design for the windows and shutters. Despite the differences in design and
function, the brickwork of the façade on Toldwarsstraat
continues in a single plane, so that the whole appears as
one complex. The vertical series of balconies opens the
block at the corners and is topped by dormer windows
reaching almost to the roof ridge. The two side walls echo
the front façade. The balconies and the prominently
designed chimneys are distinguishing elements however.

The building has undergone some changes since 1908.
The windows and entrances have been changed and the
shutters have disappeared; the tablet designed by Berlage
above the central entrance on Toldwarsstraat has also
been removed. The side wings on Pieter Aertszstraat and
Tolstraat now have another function, as a consequence of
which the entrances had to be enlarged.

Dagteeken- en Kunstambachtsschool voor Meisjes 1908
16 Gabriël Metsustraat
Function: arts and crafts school for girls
Commissioned by: board of the Dagteeken- en
Kunstambachtsschool

The façade of the school is dominated by the entrance: a portico with a semicircular arch one and a half floors high. A double door gives access to a lobby, which is lit by windows above the entrance and is still mostly in its original state. The windows of the former director's office are located above the arch of the portico. As a result of the high lobby the floor level of this is higher than that of the adjacent classrooms.

Large windows have been placed on either side of the entrance, two pairs on the left for smaller classrooms and three pairs on the right for the large classrooms. The first floor has an identical window layout. The façade is of brick, with stone at structurally important places, such as the lintels and plinth. To the left and right of the arch there is a decorative band of yellow-red brick.

In the original building the seven dormer windows separated by an almost vertical roof form a horizontal series. In significant alteration work, the character of the façade was retained as much as possible but the attic floor was extended to form a full floor. The original pitch of the roof can still be seen at the extreme left and right, though the bright red tiles have disappeared. The green-painted cast-iron railings in front of the building are still more or less in their original state.

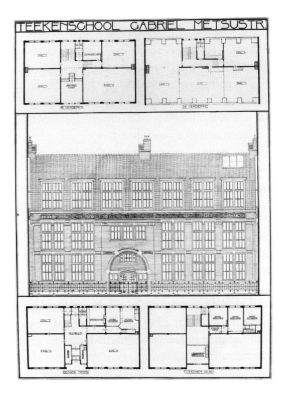

Façade

Westerspeeltuin 1908
J.J. Cremerplein
Function: covered playground
Commissioned by: Vereniging De Westerspeeltuin
Demolished

Berlage was as closely involved with the Westerspeeltuin as he was with the Oosterspeeltuin [32]. The educational goal of such societies meant that their buildings had to be carefully designed, with the result that a famous architect designed a small building that could apparently have been built even without an architect.

The original building was to be a covered playground; it consisted of a hall with storage space behind it and measured 8 x 15 metres. It is built of wood, with a border of Saint Andrew's crosses. In the front and one side wall there are double doors; the windows can be closed with removable panels or shutters. The slightly sloping roof is covered with asphalt paper. In the course of the years much was altered; a kitchen, for example, was added, and the original rectangular floor-plan was thereby changed. These alterations were carried out using simple means. Material from the bandstand, which stood in the playground until it was demolished in 1927, was used for one of the alterations.

Situation
[*c.* 1908]

Design

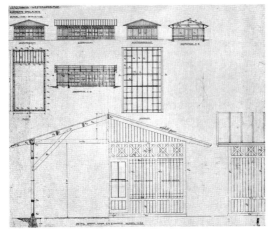

Dwellings 1908
163-213 Sarphatistraat

This long strip of residential buildings is symmetrical in structure. There is a tower at each corner and one in the middle, in the axis of Korte 's-Gravesandestraat. To the right and left of this middle, asymmetrically designed tower with a high hipped roof there are two residential buildings whose gables have been combined into one trapezium-shaped gable. Above the connected entrance arches of these houses the façade projects in the form of a bay, topped with a lean-to roof. The same motif – a trapezium-shaped gable with bay, followed by a tower – is repeated near the corners. The tower to the left has since been demolished.

The façade is rhythmically articulated between the middle and the corner towers: lower bays having an attic floor and a tiled roof are combined with flat-roofed higher bays. All the cornices rest on four protruding beams. The vertical articulation is traversed with horizontal bands of yellow brick.

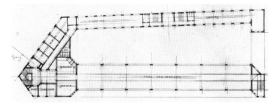

Ground-floor plan

Diamond-cutting factory date unknown
Pieter Aertszstraat
Not realized

All that exists of this design is a floor-plan for the ground floor. It is not known exactly when the design was made, though it certainly dates from before 1911-12 [see project 40, which has been built on part of the site proposed for the diamond-cutting factory]. Nor is it known why it was not built. It can be seen from the drawing that the factory was to be located in the neighbourhood of Korte Tolstraat. The floor-plan reflects the street pattern, from which it can be deduced that the entrance was envisaged on Pieter Aertszstraat. The floor-plan is elongated in form and is situated around a wide inner courtyard left open on the right towards the Toldwarsstraat side. Across from this, on the left of the inner courtyard, are the offices and entrance. The form of the floor-plan here is determined by the sharp corner formed by Pieter Aertszstraat and Tolstraat. The workshops and canteen are housed in the wings between these.

Dwellings 1912
21-53 Tolstraat
Commissioned by: Algemeene Woningbouw Vereniging

With this block of twelve residential buildings, built on the site proposed for a diamond-cutting factory [39], Berlage's role as the reformer of working-class housing began. The theme of the design is the metropolitan block in a residential district with a conventional site typology. The buildings contain some basic dwellings with living room, kitchen and two bedrooms, but apart from these Berlage also designed larger dwellings. The floor-plans of these dwellings interlock and thereby provided an alternative to the idea then current of the rented flat as something to be built on a rectangle plot with partition walls running from the front to the back. The interlocking floor-plans enable the area of a dwelling to be increased without increasing the depth of the building.

The block differs from earlier Berlage plans by the austerity of its rhythm. There are no hierarchic formal structures, no accents through axes of symmetry or picturesque irregularities. The whole is consolidated by the expressive horizontal line of the overhanging roof. All the façade motifs are arranged in the same manner next to each other under this dominating line. The dwellings are not architecturally articulated. Only five motifs determine the rhythm of the façade: two different bay forms, two sorts of window, and the balconies.

Berlage created an intermediate space between dwelling and street. The roof ridge indicates the vertical interface between street and dwelling, which permeate each other in the relief of the façade under the projecting roof. The straight plinth and the actual wall mark the course of

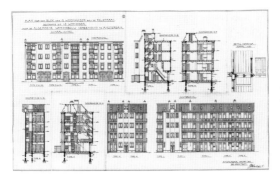

Façades and sections

the building line; it is only above the ground floor that the façade could project beyond this line, and then only slightly. To a great extent the formal development of the façade from plinth to roof determines the rhythmical effect of the alternating vertical elements. The brick bays above the entrance doors each rest on three consoles. The walls under this are made more substantial by the use of lesenes. Berlage made a brick frieze above the windows of the third floor, as a result of which the façade of the bay under the roof is almost in line with the vertical interface. The lighter wooden bays each rest on a console reinforced with a cross beam. The wall under this is flat. The top floor projects forward in its entirety, but not as far as the brick frieze. The straight wall remains present in the background. In this manner a play of light, shadow and semi-shadow in an austere rhythm is developed under the overhanging roof, which becomes contrapuntal at the ground-floor level.

Some years after the block was constructed J.C. van Epen extended it, on the basis of Berlage's plans, at the corner of Tolstraat and Pieter Aertszstraat.

Transvaalplein and surroundings 1912

Transvaalplein (formerly Transvaalstraat), Transvaalstraat,

Smitsstraat, Majubastraat, Transvaalkade (formerly Ringkade)

Function: dwellings

Commissioned by: Algemeene Woningbouw Vereniging

Berlage had already designed a building plan for the Transvaal neighbourhood in 1903. When the area came to be developed, he modified the plan in consultation with the municipality and the housing associations involved. In the case of the residential building on Tolstraat [40] it was a question of solving the problem of the street wall. In the Transvaal neighbourhood, on the other hand, the problem was much more complex because the four blocks to be built were located on three sites, two of which were already partly developed. Initially Berlage tried to bring the four blocks into a spatial relationship with each other. Through shifts in the building line and by introducing variety in the height of the buildings, he managed to achieve, on a small scale, control of the urban space. A comparison with the streets and squares in the neighbourhood makes it very clear that Berlage's three-dimensional spatial composition was far more successful than those of his colleagues.

The three residential buildings in block I on Ringkade link up with the low buildings that already stood there when this part of Amsterdam still belonged to the municipality of Nieuwer-Amstel. Berlage reinforced the rural character of the area by setting back the façades and creating space for well-situated front gardens. The buildings in block IV, on the other hand, are adapted to the metropolitan idea of Amsterdam. The residential four-storey buildings are similar in type to those developed for

Transvaal-plein

Situation

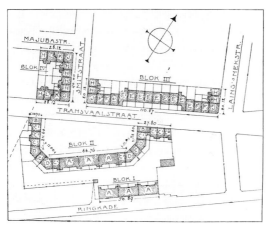

Tolstraat, though higher buildings with shops and dwellings above them are situated at the corners. The spatial interaction between these two spheres, between the urban and the rural, takes place on Transvaalstraat. The corners of block III repeat the metropolitan-block motif. On either side of the high buildings with shops, which are made even higher by the tiled roof, there are four-storey blocks. These too are 'slices', cut out of the Tolstraat block. The difference in height with the corner buildings is dramatized by the fact that the cornice begins somewhat lower and the roof is not visible from the street. The centre of block III, partly recessed in order to create space for front gardens, has three residential floors and an attic floor. This recessed row has a tiled roof, whose ridge links up with the cornice of neighbouring buildings. Opposite block III are the low-rise buildings of block II on Transvaalstraat. The first four lots are in the building line of the street, but then the row recedes to form an irregular polygonal square. The buildings at the corners of the square and street have been made somewhat higher to mark the border between the two spaces. Transvaalplein visually closes off Smitstraat. Berlage's design for the Transvaal neighbourhood as a whole met the desire often expressed at the time for closed and variegated townscapes.

Two blocks of houses in Amsterdam-Noord 1911-14
Spreeuwenpark, Sperwerlaan, Havikslaan, Leeuwerikstraat
With: J.C. van Epen
Commissioned by: Algemeene Woningbouw Vereniging

A great merit of the housing associations was the reintroduction of low-rise housing. J.H.W. Leliman was one of the first to realize such housing, in 1912 for Zeeburgerdijk, a commission from Eigen Haard. Berlage and the AWV immediately followed his example with the low-rise block on Transvaalplein [41]. Low-rise working-class housing was subsequently built on a very large scale in Amsterdam-Noord. In the vision of A. Keppler, the Director of the Housing Department, Amsterdam-Noord would be a real garden city, with single- and two-storey houses surrounded by greenery.

Berlage and van Epen continued here to build on what had been achieved in the Transvaal neighbourhood. In principle they used three floor-plans. Apart from the type already developed for the buildings on Transvaalplein and consisting of two ground-floor dwellings with three separate upper dwellings, they designed another type with two interlocking floor-plans. Here the rooms could be made broader and situated better with respect to each other. Berlage and van Epen had developed an original solution to the problem of the lower dwellings being small due to the need to provide independent access to the upper dwellings. In the third type two plots with lower and upper dwellings enclose a section 2.2 metres wide. The ground floor of this linking structure belongs to one of the two ground-floor dwellings, while the first floor is accessible from the other ground-floor dwelling. In this type all the partition walls continue up to the roof.

Situation

*Façades and
interlocked
floor-plans*

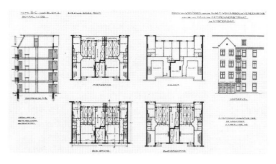

Façade and floor-plans

Housing blocks in the Staatslieden neighbourhood 1913
Van Hallstraat, Schaepmanstraat, De Kempenaerstraat
With: J.C. van Epen
Commissioned by: Algemeene Woningbouw Vereniging
Not realized

These blocks were the last Berlage designed for the AWV.
The articulation of the façade follows the already famil-
iar models but it lacks the power of his earlier works;
staircase towers, with and without gables, and series of
shallow balconies or bays help to enliven the street wall.
Berlage's plans were incomplete by the time he joined
Wm.H. Müller & Co. and moved to The Hague in 1914.
J.C. van Epen, a specialist in housing who had already
worked on the project with Berlage, took over the commission and completely revised the plans. The block he
designed in Van Hallstraat is one of the finest examples of
working-class housing of the period.

Dwellings 1911-15
Javastraat, Balistraat, Molukkenstraat
Commissioned by: De Arbeiderswoning

The association De Arbeiderswoning set itself the goal of building housing for large families unable to afford the rents usual for social housing. In 1910, when it became apparent that there would be a considerable shortage of cheap housing, the association published an elaborate plan to build 700 dwellings. A year later Berlage made a series of designs as part of this plan. For financial reasons, however, it was spring 1915 before construction work could start. The dwellings met the minimum requirements then laid down under the housing regulations: the communal stairwell provides access to eight dwellings, and instead of the kitchen there is only a scullery – to prevent people living in the kitchen and subletting the other rooms.

What is most striking about this project is the site typology. Neighbourhoods like this are characterized by elongated blocks oriented to the east and west, producing extremely monotonous streetscapes. Furthermore, almost half of the dwellings are unfavourably situated with respect to the sun. The original commission probably did not include much more than the continuation of the already half-completed block on Molukkenstraat. This was the case, for instance, with the adjoining block to the south between Balistraat and Eerste Atjehstraat, which had been designed by no less an architect than J.E. van der Pek (1912). Berlage devised an original solution however: by introducing two side streets he split the design into three blocks, situated around communal gardens. The blocks are now oriented to the north and south, and

*Façades
Molukken-
straat/
Balistraat*

Floor-plans

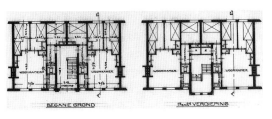

BEGANE GROND   1ste en 2de VERDIEPING

the dwellings, for the most part, are better positioned in relation to the sun and on quiet residential streets.

Also remarkable are the corner solutions. They illustrate the problem of the corner dwelling; hitherto, this problem had only been surmounted by resorting to awkward recesses in the rear elevation. Ventilation and light continued to be problematic however. Berlage found a solution that, in its simplicity, was a stroke of genius: the negative or receding corner. This discovery enriches the townscape and makes perfectly formed inner courts possible, while the floor-plan of the corner dwellings is considerably improved.

The articulation of the façades is unusually robust. The walls in the receding corner rise without a plinth out of the street surface as far as the ridge of the roof. The gutters are sharply delineated and included in the gable shoulders. Staircase bays are positioned above the entrances and their volume is linked to the block by the surrounding cornice. The roof is not interrupted by dormer windows. The impact of the vertical elements is softened somewhat by a continuous frieze, two bricks in height and at the same level as the lintels. This brick is lighter in colour and roughly worked. All the details are in brick. The complex has been extensively altered; excepting the entrance doors, the façades are still in their original state however.

Front façades

Housing block 1911-15
Gillis van Ledenberchstraat, Zaagmolenstraat, Rombout
Hogerbeetsstraat
Commissioned by: De Arbeiderswoning

This block repeats in a weakened form the layout of the blocks for De Arbeiderswoning in the Indische neighbourhood [44]. The staircase bays, which hardly protrude, interrupt the cornice and the eaves of the roof. This creates a rhythmical silhouette effect that is less monumental than in the Indische neighbourhood. Because the sloping roof is also set back and the cornice continues uninterrupted, the recess at the corner is less bold and not so sharply accentuated.

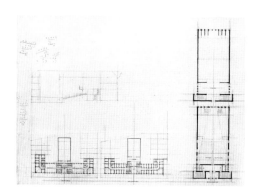

Ground-floor plan

Theatre 1898-1911
Johannes Vermeerstraat
Not realized

All that exists of this design is a floor-plan of the ground floor and a site plan. The site plan shows that the theatre was to be located on Johannes Vermeerstraat. Both drawings are undated but were probably made between 1898 and 1911 because the Velox bicycle training school indicated on the drawing was opened in 1898 and replaced by the Zuiderbad swimming pool in 1911. From the floor-plan it is possible to deduce that the building was to have another function in addition to that of a theatre. On the basis of the conference hall and dining hall, housed in two wings on either side of the actual theatre section, it is likely that it was intended to be a club or an artists' centre as well.

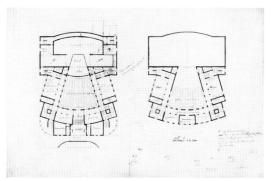

*Ground-
and first-floor
plans*

Theatre date unknown
Not realized

Two drawings were made for this theatre; both illustrate
the floor-plans of the ground floor and the first floor. They
probably belong to the same design for a Wagnertheatre.
This can be seen in the segment-shaped auditorium with
orchestra pit, which, although it is called a theatre, shows
similarities to the Wagnertheatre Berlage designed for
Scheveningen in 1910. Neither of the drawings is signed
or dated, and it is impossible to deduce for which site in
Amsterdam the design was made. One of the drawings is
provided with a commentary. It is possible that the drawings were made by one of Berlage's assistants and that
they represent more the elaboration of an idea than an
actual commission.

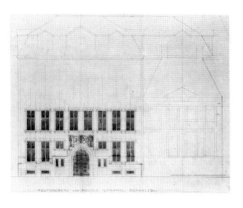

Entrance to police headquarters date unknown
185 Oudezijds Achterburgwal
Not realized

In 1913 an annexe was built to the police headquarters, located in the Oude Spinhuis on Oudezijds Achterburgwal. It was not designed by Berlage, but he later designed a new façade for the annexe. The existing façade, which Berlage apparently considered so unsuited to its function that he proposed redesigning it, is still to be seen. From the drawing it appears he was chiefly interested in the entrance. By facing the original brick wall with rustication and placing the arms of Amsterdam above the entrance, it acquires the monumental aspect Berlage thought suitable for such an important official building. The drawing is neither signed nor dated, but it was probably made shortly after 1913.

Artists' House 1912
Roelof Hartplein (formerly Roelof Hartstraat)
Function: administrative offices, office for copyright association,
conference and exhibition rooms, and a club
Commissioned by: Verbond van Nederlandsche Kunstenaars-
verenigingen
Not realized

The Verbond van Nederlandsche Kunstenaarsverenigin-
gen was founded in 1911 as an umbrella organization for
several artists' associations. Its goal was to promote the
fine arts and the interests of Dutch artists. To this end they
wanted a building in which to house an office for the
copyright association, but also to have rooms for con-
ferences, lectures, performances of music and drama, and
exhibitions. In addition, rooms were needed for an artists' club. Such aims required a monumental building in
which all these functions could be located. For this
reason Berlage was brought in as architectural advisor by
the organizing committee at an early stage. At the beginning of 1912 the Verbond published a leaflet in which the
provisional sketches and floor-plans were presented. The
original idea was to build behind the Rijksmuseum, but
when this turned out to be impossible the present-day
Roelof Hartplein was chosen for the site.

The location presented Berlage with some problems in
determining the layout of façades and floor-plans, problems concerning in particular the two components of the
building, the clubrooms and theatre, both of which required their own entrance. There was, however, only one
prominent place for an entrance, namely in the axis of
Roelof Hartstraat. Berlage designed several variations in
which he experimented with the location of the entrance

to the theatre and related this to the orientation of the auditorium within the building itself. From preliminary studies it can be seen that Berlage regarded the entrance to the auditorium as the most important. The committee, on the other hand, wanted the entrance to the club to be on the axis of Roelof Hartstraat, so Berlage was forced to rotate the entire design.

As far as the division of the building mass, the layout of the façade and the decoration was concerned, the simplest variation was chosen. In earlier designs Berlage had opted for considerable contrast between angular and round forms. In the published version the decoration consisted of various bands of relief, in contrast to the richer decoration of the earlier designs. In the version finally adopted the clubrooms were strictly separated from the theatre and the accompanying foyers. Exhibition rooms were planned on the second floor above the theatre. These could be reached by lifts. The positioning of the exhibition rooms so high in the building was determined by the desire for natural light from above. In 1914 the building was definitively cancelled for financial reasons.

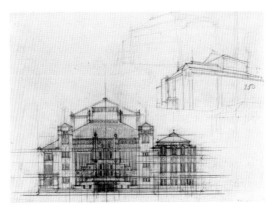

First design

Final design

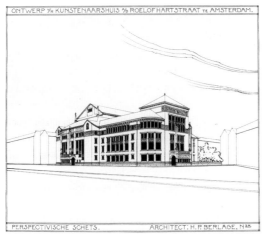

Head office Rijksverzekeringsbank 1925
Apollolaan/Stadionweg
Not realized

At the end of 1925 Berlage was commissioned to design the new head office of the Rijksverzekeringsbank, which was to form part of *Plan-Zuid*. The municipality was supposed to make a site available at the end of Ferdinand Bolstraat. There were protests from local people, however, against the choice of this street as the site for such a monumental building; the caption 'Proposal for the location of the Rijksverzekeringsbank in somewhat different surroundings' shows that an alternative site was eventually found for the building at the corner of Apollolaan and Stadionweg.

The only surviving floor-plan is that for the ground floor. Sketches of the elevations show that the building was intended to have more floors. The drawings give only a rough idea of the building Berlage had in mind though. What is clear, however, is that the form of the site was decisive in determining the layout of the floor-plan, and that the building was to be monumental and, partly due to its corner location, had to serve as a major accent in the townscape. It is unknown why the plans were not developed further. The new head office was eventually built in 1939, to a design by D. Roosenburg.

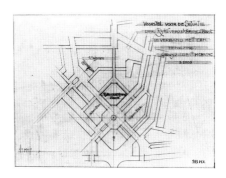

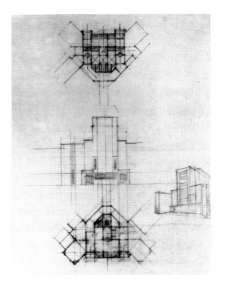

Situation

*Floor-plans
and façade*

De Amsterdamsche Bank 1926-32
47 Rembrandtplein
Function: head office and branch
With: B.J. and B.W. Ouëndag (floor-plan), L. Zijl (sculptor)
Commissioned by: De Amsterdamsche Bank

The ground floor of the current building gives an illusion of openness that makes the building inviting enough for clients to enter but is also closed enough to give the secure impression of a bank. This openness, greater than in the original design of 1926, was the result of alterations and an extension carried out in 1966. The changes were extremely far-reaching, particularly on the ground floor and top floor. They involved the use of much more glass than in the original design. The extension on the roof has considerably altered the building's outline. This plentiful use of glass and the many pavilion roofs have given the building a crystalline character. A new glass entrance on Rembrandtplein and the addition of display cases along the wall of the square and under the arcade also contributed to the combination of openness and security.

The original situation was almost completely different; in 1926 people attached more value to security and its expression than to the openness of a bank. The building was striking primarily for its enormous dimensions. Berlage was only responsible for the façades, which tower above the ground floor and have extremely large windows. Part of the façade on Utrechtsestraat projects to form an arcade. On the Rembrandtplein itself, Berlage designed a high, narrow windowless tower to the right of the entrance. The flat roof and angular contours, together with the type of material used, ensure the remarkably robust character of the building.

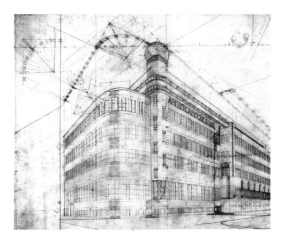

Preliminary design

Building shortly after construction

During the design process Berlage considered less formal possibilities; one involved a round corner on Rembrandt-plein and Amstelstraat and a round tower, surmounted by a globe instead of a spire. Oddly enough, by marking the entrance on Rembrandtplein with a tower it becomes more prominent than the actual main entrance on Heren-gracht. This entrance, next to the bank's original building (designed by Eduard Cuypers and demolished to make way for the extension), was in a much quieter location than Rembrandtplein, however, one more in keeping with the dignity characteristic of the main entrance to a bank in 1926. For this entrance the same reddish-pink stone is used as for the rest of the building, but for the entrance the stone is highly polished.

Buildings on Mercatorplein 1925-27
Function: dwellings and shopping arcades
Commissioned by: Bouwmaatschappij Amsterdam-West and De
Hoofdweg N V

Mercatorplein is at the centre of Plan-West, the 6000 dwellings plan submitted to the municipality in 1922 by a consortium of private builders. As a result of financial problems, construction work could only start in 1924. The architectural supervision of this plan, on which all the well-known architects of the Amsterdam School worked, was in the hands of J. Gratama, G. Versteeg and A.R. Hulshof, a director within the Department of Public Works. The architectural bureau of Gulden & Geldmaker carried out the design. Berlage designed the layout of Mercatorplein, the façades and the two towers. The tower in the north-east corner has been demolished.

The square is bordered by shops; these are either in the form of covered arcades or under projecting awnings. In this way the residents above the shops are relatively undisturbed. The centre blocks on the long sides of the square are somewhat higher than the buildings at the corners. The façade is set back and the square is thereby optically enlarged. The three series of linked balconies contrast with the strict articulation of the bay windows to the left and right, and, similarly, the massive pillars contrast with the long shadow under the awnings, which make the recessed ground floor almost invisible. The short façades of the square are staggered with respect to each other and have been designed asymmetrically. Here the two gateway towers have also been recessed, and the northern and southern façades appear to project as a result. The length of the square is thus optically reduced.

Mercatorplein is a so-called turbine square: all the streets end in a façade or a gateway. This form gives the square a closed appearance, but traffic is not much impeded. Berlage had originally designed a monumental gateway in the western façade of the square; this was supposed to visually close off Jan Evertsenstraat. The plan was not realized, however; instead, the street profile is narrowed by two extensions to suggest closure.

With Mercatorplein Berlage's ideal of a people's square – which had already influenced his two extension plans for the south of Amsterdam – was realized, though to a limited extent. In both the first and second *Plan-Zuid* Berlage had designed a people's palace on a large square, on the site of what later became the first RAI exhibition centre. It was never built, but Berlage persevered nevertheless. In one of his earliest designs for Mercatorplein the entire block on the eastern side is reserved for a 'people's palace', a sort of 'Stadtkrone'.

Mercator-plein seen from the south-west [tower now demolished]

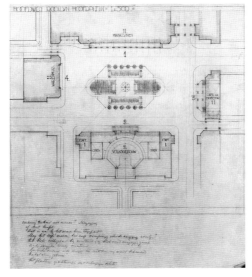

Situation, Mercator-plein with people's palace

Berlagebrug 1926-32
Continuation of Vrijheidslaan (formerly Amstellaan)
With: C. Biemond, H. Krop (sculptor)
Commissioned by: Department of Public Works, city of Amsterdam

The complex known as the Berlagebrug consists of more than just the bridge over the Amstel. Both the buildings on the bank along Weesperzijde and Amsteldijk to the north of the bridge and the Schollenbrug over the Ringvaart form part of Berlage's design. Because of the short distance between the bridge over the Amstel and the Schollenbrug it was necessary to connect them, which meant that the quay on Weesperzijde had to be raised three metres. Berlage used the raised quay for boathouses. As with the Nieuwe Amstelbrug [28], Berlage was asked to revise a design drawn up by the city's Department of Public Works. Nothing has been changed in the layout of their design; only the boathouses have been added.

The design is visually dominated by the off-centre tower, which provides shelter for the bridgemaster and houses electrical equipment. It has become a sturdy, angular tower, somewhat unapproachable, narrowing as it rises up out of the water from its stone base. The small windows emphasize its stern character, one worthy of a watchtower. A female figure has been placed on the tower looking out over the water towards Amsterdam. She represents the Genius, the tutelary spirit of Amsterdam, and stands above three green bands representing the canals. The statue was designed by H. Krop in collaboration with Berlage.

The bridge itself consists of five bays, with the middle one built as a single bascule bridge, the moveable part of

Tower, part of the bridge

which is on the axis of the water. The asymmetry of the single bascule bridge immediately attracted Berlage. He stuck to his view that bridges can tolerate little decoration: the appearance of the bridge is therefore determined by the use of unusual materials. The largest part of the structure is made from red Limburg brick, finished with yellow Bavarian granite. The supporting structures of the bridge spans are faced with green-glazed brick. The parapets are made of cast iron with a top rail of tombac. Like the cast-iron lampposts and tram masts, they are painted red and black (the colours of Amsterdam).

Although the bridge across the Amstel is the main feature, the whole complex is conspicuous for the unity of form and use of materials. Berlage saw the bridge as an architectural conclusion to the actual city. Beyond this, the new city and countryside began; the bridge was a signpost indicating the Amstel's transition from urban waterway to country river. This idea was expressed by 'embracing' the area of the river by the architecture of the bridge and the buildings on both banks, and it was also emphasized by the tower. The bridge was incorporated in Berlage's *Plan-Zuid*, its position being determined by the axis of Amstellaan.

The bridge was opened in 1932, though, on account of the economic crisis in the early 1930s, work on the pavilion, which was to have terraces on Amsteldijk and an uninterrupted view across the Amstel towards the city, was postponed for some time. It had been designed by Berlage in the same style as the bridge, but his design was never realized. The present-day clubhouse was built by J.J. van der Linden in 1953.

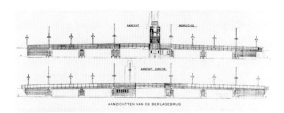

Sketches

Design for a pavilion [not realized]

Plan for two squares in the south of Amsterdam 1929
Allebéplein (currently intersection of Apollolaan and Minervalaan),
Minervaplein
With: A. Bruinsma
Competition entry, *not realized*

In the course of the 1920s Amsterdam too was influenced
by the trend towards high-rise building that affected
many European cities after the First World War. Property
developers, the construction industry, architects' organizations and also political parties criticized Amsterdam's
building regulations, which limited the height of new
housing development to a maximum of four storeys. In
1925 therefore the mayor and aldermen were urgently
requested to submit proposals for the revision of these
regulations. At the end of 1928 the city council debated
the question of building height after the publication of a
preliminary recommendation concerning building height
by the mayor and aldermen. It decided that, in order to
improve the aesthetic quality of the city, higher buildings
should be permitted in certain locations than was currently possible under the regulations. As a result of this
decision, J.F. Staal's 'Wolkenkrabber' on Victorieplein,
the plans for which had been ready for a long time, was
finally built. The decision also made possible the higher
buildings on Minervaplein by C.J. Blaauw (1932). In the
course of the debate, the city council decided to organize
a competition for Minervaplein and Allebéplein, and not
to exclude high-rise buildings on principle. The two large
squares lie across the axis of Minervalaan. Berlage and
Bruinsma accentuated the short sides of the two squares
by tower blocks with varying forms. The façades of the
squares are mainly five-storey high.

Tower block, south-east corner of Allebéplein

*Portrait of
Berlage by
Chris Lebeau
[1912]*

1856   Born in Amsterdam, 21 February

1875-78   Studied architecture at the Eidgenössische Technische
          Hochschule in Zurich

1879-80   Worked in Frankfurt

1880-81   Travelled to Germany, Austria and Italy

1881   Established himself in Amsterdam; joined bureau of
          Th. Sanders

1889   Independent practice in Amsterdam

1911   Travelled to United States of America

1913   Joined the firm of Wm.H. Müller & Co.; moved to The Hague
          the following year

1914   Honorary doctorate Rijksuniversiteit Groningen

1919   Independent practice in The Hague

1923   Travelled to Dutch East Indies

1924   Honorary doctorate Technische Hogeschool Delft

1934   Died in The Hague, 12 August

Dr. H.P. Berlage en zijn werk (with contributions by K.P.C. de Bazel,
    J. Gratama, J.E. van der Pek, R.N. Roland Holst, J.F. Staal,
    A. Verwey and W. Vogelzang), Rotterdam 1916.

H.P. Berlage bouwmeester 1856-1934 (with contributions by M. Bock
    and P. Singelenberg), exhibition catalogue Haags Gemeente-
    museum, The Hague 1975.

Bock, M., *Anfänge einer neuen Architektur. Berlages Beitrag zur
    architektonischen Kultur der Niederlande im ausgehenden
    19. Jahrhundert*, The Hague and Wiesbaden 1983.

Fanelli, G., *Moderne architectuur in Nederland 1900-1940*,
    The Hague 1978.

Gratama, J., *Dr. H.P. Berlage bouwmeester*, Rotterdam 1925.

*Nederlands Kunsthistorisch Jaarboek 1974 (H.P. Berlage 1856-1934.
    Een bouwmeester en zijn tijd*, Bussum 1975) (with contributions
    by M. Boot, F.F. Fraenkel, G. Hoogewoud, H. Searing and
    P. Singelenberg).

Polano, S. *Hendrik Petrus Berlage: Complete Works*, New York 1988.

Reinink, A.W., *Amsterdam en de Beurs van Berlage, reacties van
    tijdgenoten*, The Hague 1975.

Singelenberg, P., *H.P. Berlage*, Amsterdam 1969.

Singelenberg, P., *H.P. Berlage. Idea and Style. The Quest for Modern
    Architecture*, Utrecht 1972.

For sources and literature about specific subjects, buildings and
urban plans, see especially the publications by Bock, Fanelli, Polano
and Singelenberg.

All illustrations have been provided by the Dutch Architectural
Institute with the exception of:

Architectura, August 1909: p. 135

Architectura, 8 April 1916: p. 109

H.P. Berlage en zijn werk, Rotterdam 1916: p. 105

Gratama, J., *Dr. H.P. Berlage bouwmeester*, Rotterdam 1925: pp. 55,
    125 (above)

Bouwkundig Weekblad, 16 October 1897: p. 87

Bouwkundig Weekblad Architectura, 28 May 1932: pp. 167,
    169 (above)

Historisch topografische atlas Gemeentearchief Amsterdam: pp. 61,
    69, 75, 99, 111, 137 (above), 143 (above), 161 (lower)

LEGEND